Old World, New World 1480–1600

Chris Jordan
Queen Elizabeth's School and Community College, Crediton

Tim Wood

John Murray

HISTORY IN ACTION Chris Jordan and Tim Wood

Already published
England in the Middle Ages
The Ancient World

In preparation
The Modern World: 1914–1980

Acknowledgements

Artwork
All artwork (including front cover (top right) and back cover (map)) drawn by Ed Dovey.

Illustrations
American Museum of Natural History, 22, 23 (left and bottom right), 24 (left and centre), 26, 31, 34 (bottom), 37 (centre), 43 (top right); Archiv fur Kunst und Geschichte, Berlin, 46; BBC Hulton Picture Library, 7, 53 (top right), 54 (bottom), 63 (bottom), 64 (centre); Bibliothéque Nationale de Paris, 14 (top), 20, 45 (bottom); Bodleian Library, 32 (top); Courtauld Institute of Art, 50; The Fotomas Index, 18, 23 (top right), 32 (bottom), 34 (centre), 36, 38, 39, 44, 52; John Carter Brown Library, 35; John Freeman & Co., 28, 33, 40, 41, 45 (top), 47 (top), 53 (top right), cover (left); the Mansell Collection, 4, 64 (top); Mary Evans Picture Library, 12; National Maritime Museum, 21, 57, 62 (top), 63 (top); Robert Estall, 14 (bottom); Science Museum, 6, cover (bottom right); University of Utah Press, 34 (top), 37 (top); Weidenfeld (Publishers) Ltd, 48; Wellcome Institute for the History of Medicine, 54 (top).

Sources for quoted passages
p. 5: Pasqualigo, quoted in J. A. Williamson, *Voyages of the Cabots* (CUP).

p. 6: Document B by Madriaga, *Christopher Columbus* (A. P. Watt/ Collins Knowlton-Wing Inc.); Documents C, D, E, F, G, H, by Cabot, *Ordinances for the direction of the intended voyage to Cathay* quoted in Hakluyt, *Voyages and Discoveries* (Penguin).

p. 7: Document I quoted in John Ray, *Discovery and Exploration* (HEB); Document J by Richard Braithewaite, *Whimsies, or New Cast of Characters*, quoted in Ray; Document K by Jean Mocquet, quoted in Ray.

p. 12: Per Collinder, *A History of Marine Navigation* (Batsford) quoted in Richard Armstrong, *The Early Mariners* (Ernest Benn).

p. 18: Document A by Madriaga; Document B quoted in L. A. Vigneras, *The Journal of Christopher Columbus*, trans. Cecil Jane (Hakluyt Society).

pp. 21, 26, 27: Bernal Diaz, *The Conquest of New Spain* (Penguin).

p. 51: quoted in Emmison, *Elizabethan Life and Disorder* (ERO).

p. 52: W. Harrison, *The Description of Britaine*, quoted in *History Alive Source Book* (Hart Davis).

p. 64: 'The Miraculous Victory achieved by the English fleet upon the Spanish huge Armada sent in the year 1588 for the invasion of England' in Emanuel van Meteren, *History of the Low Countries*, quoted in Hakluyt.

British Library Cataloguing in Publication Data

Jordan, Chris
   Old world, new world 1480–1600
   Students' book
   1. History
   I. Title   II. Wood, Tim
   900   D21

ISBN 0–7195–3956–0

Jordan, Chris
   Old world, new world 1480–1600
   Teachers' book
   1. History
   I. Title   II. Wood, Tim
   900   D21

ISBN 0–7195–4096–8

First published 1987
by John Murray (Publishers) Ltd
50 Albemarle Street, London W1X 4BD

Reprinted 1988

Printed and bound in Great Britain at The Bath Press, Avon

Contents

The World in 1480

Venice

Europe in 1480

The map shows the world as Europeans knew it in 1480. They did not know the true shape of the world. Few had travelled into the 'unknown' areas.

Italian cities such as Venice, Genoa and Florence had grown rich through trade. Valuable luxury goods came across Asia by camel. Italian merchants carried the goods in their own ships on the last leg of the long journey across the Mediterranean to Europe.

One writer described the goods carried in Venetian ships: 'From India they have pearles, precious stones and plenty of spices . . . they have a very large quantity of cotton and silk'.

In 1453, Constantinople had been captured by the Turks, and the Turkish Empire grew. No goods from Asia could get to Europe without passing through hostile Arab or Turkish land. The Turks began to tax this trade. Luxury goods became very expensive or impossible to buy.

Powerful European leaders had good reasons to pay explorers to go on voyages to find *new trade routes* to Cathay and the Spice Islands in the Far East.

Spices

Spices from the Far East were very valuable. Cinnamon, nutmeg, cloves and ginger were used as medicines and for flavouring the boring and salty food most Europeans ate. At one time an ounce of pepper was worth the same as an ounce of gold.

Luxuries

Other luxury goods like cotton, silk, pearls, precious metals and jewels flowed into Europe. Italian merchants became very rich.

Religion

The Catholic Church was looking for new converts. Most Catholic expeditions carried priests with them.

Ambition

Many sea captains were ambitious and saw a chance to make lots of money and become famous. They were helped by the new technology of the time. This had produced better ships, navigation aids and guns. These developments made the voyages much more likely to succeed.

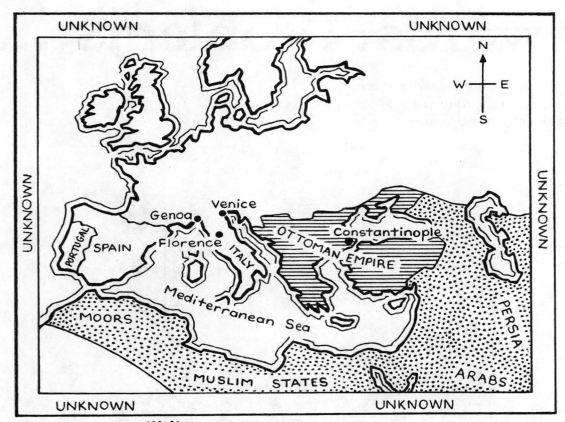

UNKNOWN UNKNOWN

N
W E
S

UNKNOWN

UNKNOWN

PORTUGAL
SPAIN
Genoa
Venice
Florence
ITALY
OTTOMAN EMPIRE
Constantinople
PERSIA
Mediterranean Sea
MOORS
MUSLIM STATES
ARABS

UNKNOWN

UNKNOWN

·:·:·: Cuts off Europe from trade with Asia

*Description of a successful
captain, John Cabot*

'He is called the Great Admiral, and vast honour is
paid to him, and he goes dressed in silk, and these
English run after him like mad, and indeed he can en-
list as many of them he pleases.'

Goods coming from the Far East in 1480

Spices	Jewels	Cloth	Metals	Others

China—coral—sandalwood—
lacquer—musk—silk—amber—
quicksilver—copper—mace—
white pepper—ginger—silver—
carpets—cloves—nutmeg—gold—
cloth of gold—sugar—alum—
rosewater—vermillion—pearls—
wax—ivory

1 Look at the picture of Venice opposite. What clues can you find that it was a rich and powerful city?

2 Copy the table above (yours will be bigger). Put each of the trade goods mentioned into the right column.

3 Which group of goods can no longer be thought of as luxury goods?

4 Write 2 sentences explaining how the capture of Constantinople by the Turks affected Venice.

5 Explain why each of the following might have been interested in finding a new route to the Far East. The Pope—an Italian merchant—a German peasant.

6 Read the document. What extra benefit did a successful captain gain from a voyage?

7 Imagine you are the captain. Write a speech to give to a group of sailors you want to recruit as your crew on a voyage to find a new trade route to the Far East.

Rewards, Problems....

Look at the following pieces of evidence carefully. Most of them date from before 1500. Then answer the questions.

A

Martin Alonso recruits men for Columbus

B To some he said they would be raised above their poverty; to others that they would find there houses with tiles of gold; to some he offered good fortune, and for every man he had pleasant words and money; so that with this and the general trust in him, many people followed him from the towns.

John Cabot describes his destination

C ... the islands are fertile of cloves, nutmegs, mace, and cinnamon; and that the said islands, with other there about abound with gold, rubies, diamonds, jacynths, and other stones and pearls ... it was discovered that these islands set nothing by gold, but set more by a knife and a nail of iron ... and likewise the pieces of glass that we have counterfeited [faked] are as precious to them as to us their stones.

Rules for Cabot's sailors

D No blaspheming of God, or detestable swearing be used in any ship, nor communication of ribaldry, filthy tales, or ungodly talk to be suffered in the company of any ship, neither dicing, carding, tabling nor other devilish games.

E No liquor to be spilt on the ballast, nor filthiness to be left within board: the cook room, and all other places to be kept clean for the better health of the company.

F Not to disclose to any nation the state of our religion, but to pass it over in silence, without any declaration of it, seeming to bear with such laws and rites, as the place hath, where you shall arrive.

G For as much as our people, and ships may appear unto them strange and wondrous, and theirs also to ours: it is to be considered how they may be used, learning much of their natures and dispositions, by some one such person, as you may first either allure, or take to be brought on board your ships, and there to learn as you may, without violence or force. The person so taken to be well entertained, and ... made drunk with your beer, or wine, you shall know the secrets of his heart.

H Every nation is to be considered advisedly, and not to provoke them by any disdain, laughing, contempt, or suchlike, but to use them with prudent circumspection, with all gentleness, and courtesy.

....and Dangers

**How others saw the explorers
(written after 1500 by a Chinese person);**

I They are greedy and cunning and know a lot about valuable merchandise. They are very clever in making gain. They will risk their lives for profit and no place is too far away for them to visit ... If they come across you at sea they are certain to rob you.

Problems

J ... with the heat and dampness, our ship biscuit had become so wormy that, God help me, I saw many who waited for darkness to eat the porridge made of it that they might not see the maggots.

**A Frenchman describes the scurvy—
a disease caused by a lack of vitamin C:**

K It rotted my gums, which gave out black and putrid blood. My thighs and lower legs were black and had gangrene and I was forced to use my knife each day to cut into the flesh in order to release this black and foul blood.

L

1 Bad air and rubbish below decks caused lung disease. Sailors often hit their heads on low beams. They could be crushed by loose cargoes in storms. Bad food and water caused fever and other illnesses.

2 On deck a loose gun could crush sailors. Limbs could be cut off by snapping cables. Injuries caused by lifting heavy weights or pulling on ropes were common.

3 In storms sailors often fell onto the deck and were killed or drowned after falling into the sea. They might also be struck by lightning.

1 Which pieces of evidence show there was great wealth to be won by travellers?

2 Which piece of evidence shows that volunteers may have been taken in by exaggerated stories?

3 Which 2 pieces of evidence put forward sensible precautions to be taken on board to avoid trouble or illness among the sailors?

4 Which 2 pieces of evidence show that drunkenness could be a problem on a ship? Give 2 reasons why this could cause trouble.

5 Which 4 pieces of evidence hint that the travellers might not be honest or fair with strangers they meet?

6 Which 2 pieces of evidence show sensible precautions to avoid annoying strangers?

7 How does Cabot say his crew should behave towards people with a different religion? Why?

8 What will foreigners think of the explorers?

9 Who will benefit most from voyages of exploration? Who will benefit least?

10 Imagine you are the mother of a young man who has been asked to go on a voyage into unknown seas. Write a conversation with him in which you give all the reasons why you do not want him to go.

11 You have been offered the chance to go on a voyage. Will you go? Say why (or why not).

The Ship....

It is 1486. You are a skilful sailor who has come to Castile in Spain to seek adventure. You have heard that a number of captains have made successful voyages into unknown parts of the world. They have returned with great wealth in the form of gold and spices.

You have joined a famous captain who intends to go on a voyage of discovery. Queen Isabella of Castile has promised him half of the money needed for the voyage. He has also been given 3 ships. He has been told to 'discover and acquire islands and mainlands in the Ocean Sea'.

If the captain is successful, he will be made Viceroy of the Western Seas. All gold, silver and spices discovered will be shared with the queen. If the captain fails, he will have to pay all the expenses of the voyage.

The flagship of the little fleet is shown in the picture. The captain now needs a crew. A good crew is essential for the success of the voyage. The crew will share one-fifth of the profits. You have been given the job of selecting the crew.

---

1 Write 3 sentences describing the sort of qualities you will look for in your crew. You can choose some words from the list below to help you. You may want to add other words of your own:

brave—kind—healthy—sensitive—strong— clever—big—small—young—experienced— married—quick-tempered—reliable—steady.

2 Design a poster which will be put up around town to recruit a crew. The poster should have a picture, a large heading which will attract volunteers, and a description of the sort of people who would be suitable for a dangerous and exciting voyage into the unknown.

3 Read this description of the captain and decide which of his qualities will be useful and which might cause problems. Say whether you think your voyage is likely to be successful.

He comes from Genoa in Italy. He studied mathematics and astronomy at university. He has sailed on voyages to the Arctic, England and the Atlantic. He was shipwrecked off Portugal in 1476.

He is vain, arrogant and boastful. His plans have already been rejected by the rulers of Genoa, England and Portugal. His wife died recently and he has a 5-year-old son.

17 Mariners

Leading seamen steer and use compass. Seamen do the work. Apprentice seamen learning the trade.

6 Other Crew

Stewards, boys and pages help the cook, run errands and take messages.

....and the Crew

4 The whole crew has been chosen but you need one more person for the Afterguard. Four people have volunteered. Read about them, describe the good and bad points about each, then choose 1 to come on the voyage. All can read and write.

A A Knight who has fought bravely in many wars. Now very poor but has travelled widely and is full of good stories. Drinks rather heavily but is good-humoured.

B A jeweller and watchmaker who is a skilled clockmaker. He can identify precious metals, and can also paint quite well.

C A merchant who is bankrupt. There is a suspicion that he fiddled the accounts. Experienced in handling money and records. He is in poor health.

D A mapmaker who believes the world is round but that the Indies are inhabited by giants. He is blind in one eye but very talkative.

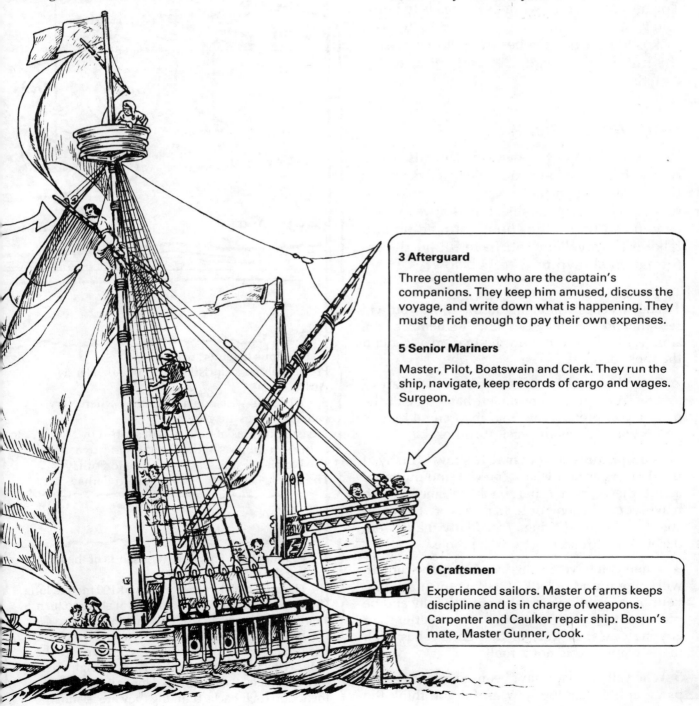

3 Afterguard

Three gentlemen who are the captain's companions. They keep him amused, discuss the voyage, and write down what is happening. They must be rich enough to pay their own expenses.

5 Senior Mariners

Master, Pilot, Boatswain and Clerk. They run the ship, navigate, keep records of cargo and wages. Surgeon.

6 Craftsmen

Experienced sailors. Master of arms keeps discipline and is in charge of weapons. Carpenter and Caulker repair ship. Bosun's mate, Master Gunner, Cook.

The Captain's Map

The captain has his ship, crew and money. He now needs a map showing the route to the legendary lands of Cathay, Cipango or the Spice Islands. Unfortunately, maps at this time were very inaccurate. They were based on rumours and guesswork rather than on accurate calculation.

Inaccurate maps

The aim of the following exercises is to show you how inaccurate maps were in 1486. Your task is to produce the best map you can from the information available, and sell it to the captain.

Travellers' tales

You have a map of the world which is based on the best ideas and travellers' tales at this time. The captain has asked you to mark on this map as many details of the known world as you can find. After hours of reading and talking to travellers you have found the information shown in **A** to **D** below.

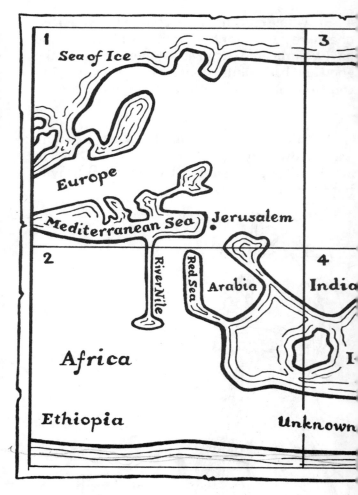

1 Your teacher will give you the route you will recommend to the captain. Remember the simplest-looking route on the map may contain the most dangers.

2 Copy the map (the bigger the better). Squares 7 and 8 can be placed on the left-hand side of the map if you prefer. The final map should show your own route as the easiest route.

3 Draw pictures on your map to show as many of the dangers as you wish. You can find out more about these from other books. Remember to make your chosen route look easier. Draw on some of the good things too. Many maps were decorated with scenes from the Bible.

4 When you have finished your map the captain will come round to look at it. You must sell him your map. Think your route out carefully and be prepared to explain why your map is better than anyone else's. Be careful though, he has seen many maps and is not a fool!

5 When all the maps have been examined write a paragraph explaining how useful you think the map will actually be to the captain.

A Fabulous legends such as:
Prester John—a Christian ruler of a rich land in Africa.
Spice Islands—islands near Cathay where very valuable spices are grown.
Treasure houses of Cathay—described by Marco Polo as the storehouses of the Great Khan's treasure.
The North-West Passage—a route to Cathay.
The North-East Passage—a route to Cathay.

B Sea monsters. There are thousands of these. Among the most feared are:
The Hydra which is a serpent about 100 metres long. These creatures throw themselves at ships to turn them over. Especially troublesome in northern seas.
The huge fish. These have been seen near Iceland. They sometimes play with barrels thrown into the water. They will overturn ships unless frightened off with trumpets. Sailors are in danger if they drop anchor on their backs thinking they are islands.

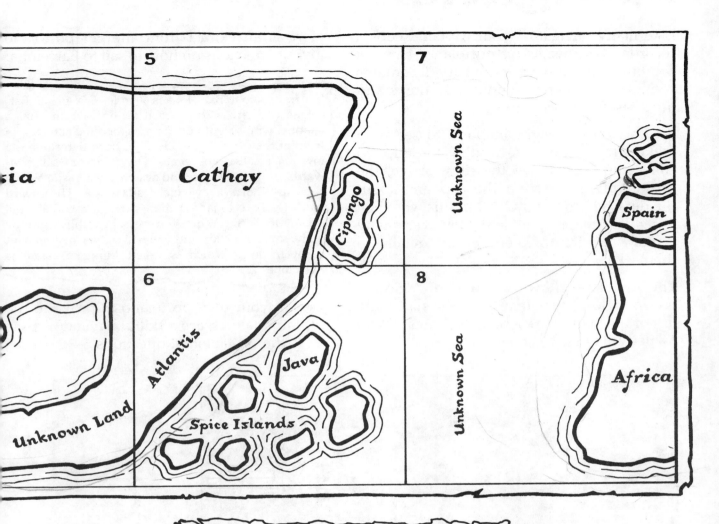

C **Natural dangers** such as: storms, fog, calms, reefs, rocks, currents, winds, heat, cold, icebergs.

D Other monsters

ANIMAL	PLACE	DESCRIPTION
Bonnacon	Asia	Has a bull's head, a horse's mane and curling horns. When chased it produces dung which burns whatever it touches
Marsok	Asia	A beast with 4 feet—2 webbed, 2 clawed; able to change its colour.
Unknown	Europe	A bird with a goose's head, the body of a crane and the feet of a calf. Buries its head in the sand when chased.
Manticora	Unknown	Lion's body, scorpion's tail and human face with triple row of teeth. Eats human flesh. Three poison stings in its tail.
Wolfman	Unknown	Human with wolf's head. Cannibal.
Cyclops	Unknown	Giant with one eye. Cannibal.

Navigation

Like many navigators your captain keeps a record of his voyage in a portolano. This is a combination of a chart and a diary. It contains compass directions, depths, tide flows and other useful information.

It is a common sight in ports to see map makers (cartographers) waiting for ships to come into port. When the ships arrive, the cartographers question the captains about the details of their voyages. In this way they bring their maps up to date. However, many captains prefer to keep certain details to themselves.

The portolano shown below is of Africa. If you look closely you may be able to spot some important landmarks and bearings. Who owned this map?

Here is an extract from another portolano giving directions on how to sail to Barcelona:

'. . . from Salo to Barcelona is 60 miles E.N.E.¼E. Barcelona is a city with a beach facing east and has a channel with a depth of 22 paces (about 30 metres) in front of the city. To the S.E. to S. from Barcelona is a low place called Lobregato. On going out sail eastwards from the shore and watch for a castle which rises up out of a valley which leads to Salo. The inward mark for Barcelona is a high steep and solitary hill called Monserrat. When you are N.E. of this, continue in the same direction and you will sight a low hill with a tower on it which is called Mongich. Here is Barcelona . . .'

Design your own portolano to prove to the captain that you are a skilful navigator. Base it on the problems in questions 6–12.

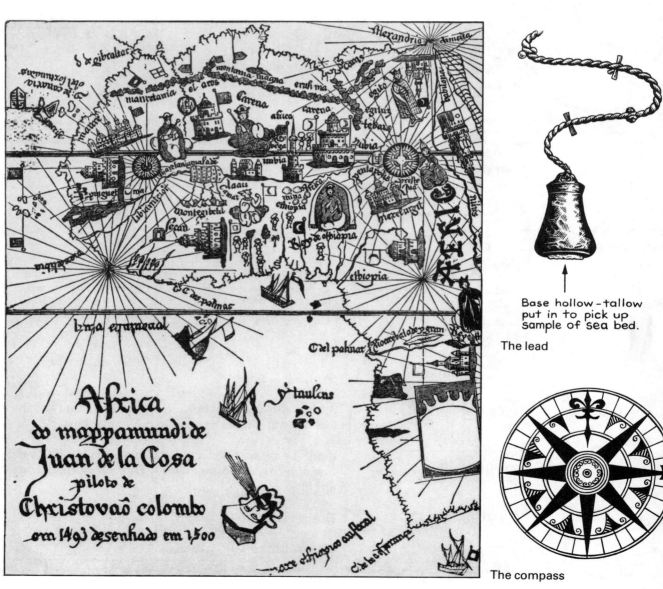

Base hollow – tallow put in to pick up sample of sea bed.

The lead

The compass

1 What is the first landmark to look for when entering Barcelona harbour?

2 What are the 2 landmarks that guide you to Barcelona itself?

3 Would this portolano be more, or less, useful to a captain than the map on pages 10 and 11? Give your reasons.

4 Suggest why captains often kept their portolanos secret, even writing them in code.

5 How was the lead used?

6 Your ship, the 'Golden Venture', is exploring an uncharted coast. You leave island A on 3rd January, sail without stopping, alter course several times, then discover an unknown, uninhabited landing place ('Port Venture') on 8th February. Bad weather causes your records to be incomplete. Port Venture is one of the places marked 1–8 on the map. Your task is to calculate which one it is. Use the map and the table to work it out.

7 Copy out the table and fill in all the spaces marked 'unknown' with the correct measurements.

8 Copy the map and mark your course from island A to Port Venture.

9 Draw a sketch of Port Venture from the sea marking any landmarks, dangerous rocks etc. This must be a sketch from your ship, not a map or plan. Use the example at the bottom of the page to guide you. Make notes on the correct and safe way to enter the harbour. As you are the only person who has discovered Port Venture, you will have to make up your own details.

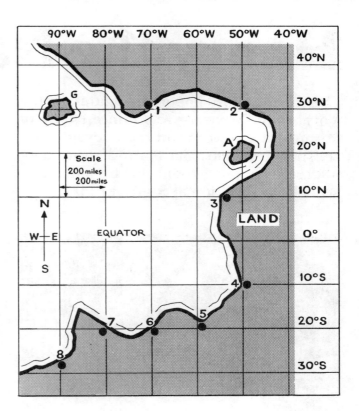

10 Using the document on the opposite page as a guide, give clear sailing instructions for a *direct* route from island G to Port Venture.

11 On your portolano, draw pictures and write descriptions of the wonderful, strange animals and plants you saw as well as the spices and other valuable goods you found. (Nobody except you knows about these.)

12 Arrange a class exhibition of portolanos. You can add lots of other details about your voyage and the monsters you saw.

STAGE	STARTING DATE	COURSE	DISTANCE TRAVELLED	ENDING LATITUDE	ENDING LONGITUDE
A–B	3 Jan.	S.W.	unknown	10°N.	unknown
B–C	6 Jan.	S.	200 miles	unknown	60°W.
C–D	16 Jan.	unknown	200 miles	10°S.	60°W.
D–E	21 Jan.	W.	unknown	10°S.	80°W.
E–F	31 Jan.	S.E.	unknown	unknown	unknown

A = Island A; F = Port Venture.

Thus Sheweth Dartmouth when it beareth W.N.W. 2 miles

13

Henry the Navigator....

One of the most important figures in the Voyages of Discovery was Prince Henry of Portugal. He never went on a voyage himself, but he tried to make Portugal the leading seafaring nation. He did this by building a school of navigation at Sagres in 1421.

Henry the Navigator

Sagres

Henry invited experts there from all over the world. Astronomers and mathematicians from as far away as Arabia came to exchange ideas and teach Henry's sailors. Among the achievements of Henry's school were:

1 Accurate charts with lines of latitude on them.
2 The first accurate tables of the angles of the sun, which greatly helped the calculation of latitude.
3 A chart-making school set up by Jafuda, the son of Abraham Cresques, the greatest chartmaker of the time.
4 Many new portolanos.
5 New and accurate navigation instruments. Some of these were based on Arab instruments used for long overland journeys. The 2 most important were the astrolabe and the cross-staff (see pictures opposite).

Henry encouraged his captains in every way he could. He allowed shipbuilders free wood from the royal forests. Materials for building ships could be imported without any taxes.

Henry believed that all this would give Portugal a world lead in exploration. What went on at Sagres was a closely guarded secret. The loss of a chart from Sagres would cost a captain his life. Captains were trained to falsify their records. However, the secrets of routes to new countries did emerge slowly. This was because the Portuguese had no deep-water sailors of their own. So they had to hire foreigners who found out the secret routes.

Henry also laid down strict rules of behaviour for sailors. Here are some of them:

1 A ship's clerk who makes false records to be branded and lose his right hand.
2 A sailor falling asleep on watch to be put on a diet of bread and water. (If the offence occurs in enemy waters, he must be stripped, flogged by his messmates and ducked 3 times.)
3 An officer falling asleep on watch to have a bucket of water thrown over his head.

and the Barrier of Fear

The African coast between Cape Non and Cape Bojador is sinister. The sea is coloured red by sand blown off the desert. There are strong currents which cause many ship-wrecks. The coast is a desolate waste of sand dunes. In 1430 the Portuguese were afraid of Cape Bojador. They believed that to the south lay a green sea of darkness, an area of fog and currents from which there was no return. Further south lay regions so hot that blood would boil and no one could live.

Henry believed there was a route to Cathay around the south of Africa. However, if this was to be discovered, Portuguese sailors must pass Cape Bojador. Henry sent out at least 14 captains with instructions to pass Cape Bojador, but they all failed. Eventually, in 1433, Henry sent his own shield-bearer, Gil Eannes. He failed to pass the cape on his first voyage, but in 1434, he made the journey again. This time he took a wide loop to the west and was successful. Once he had passed Cape Bojador, the route to the south lay open.

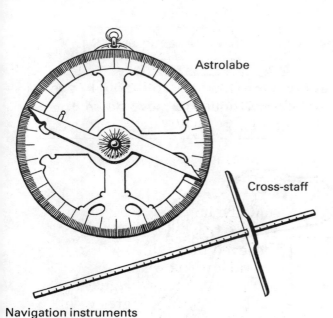

Astrolabe

Cross-staff

Navigation instruments

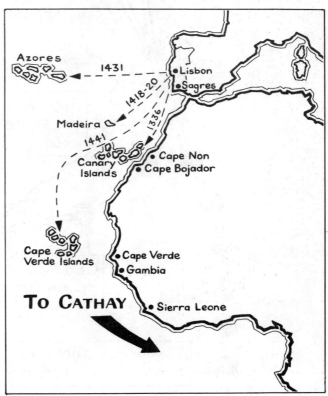

1 You have been given the job of writing about Henry the Navigator in the Encyclopaedia Anglica. Write about his main achievements in not more than 100 words.

2 Why were rules for sailors so strict? What might have happened if discipline on board had been slack?

3 Suggest what punishment might have been given for serious offences like mutiny or murder; and for less serious offences like stealing and swearing.

4 Explain in your own words why passing Cape Bojador was so important for the Portuguese.

5 Here are 3 reasons which different people might have given to explain why Cape Bojador seemed impassable. Match the person to the reason.

PERSON	REASON
1 Henry to his wife Philippa	(a) Cape Bojador was a magical point beyond which no ship could pass.
2 One of Henry's captains	(b) The weather south of Cape Bojador was so hot that humans would die.
3 A sailor in an alehouse	(c) Cape Bojador was near the Canary Islands where large amounts of valuable goods could be bought cheaply.

15

A Portuguese Voyage

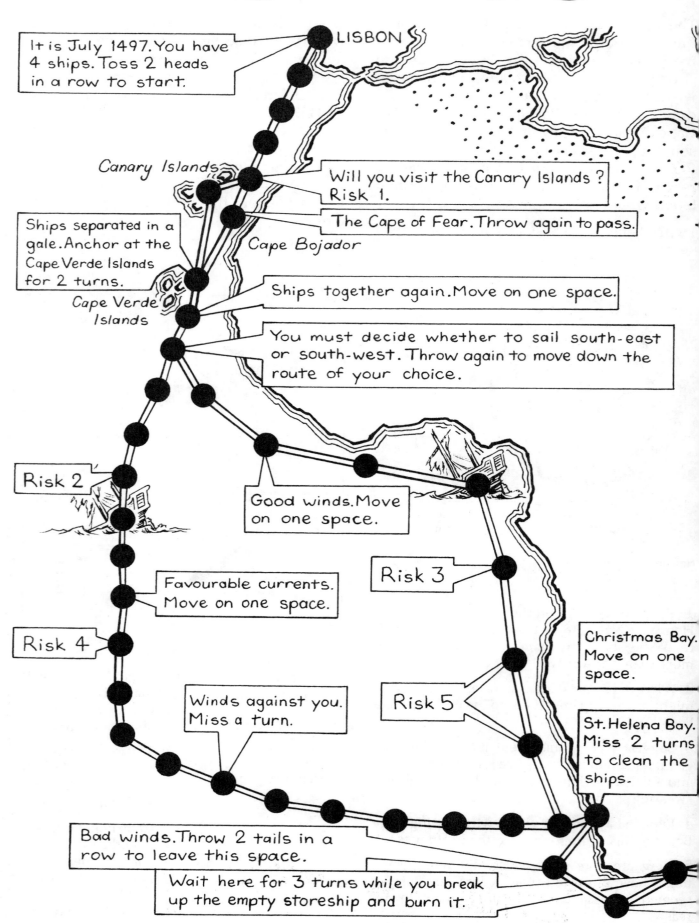

LISBON

It is July 1497. You have 4 ships. Toss 2 heads in a row to start.

Canary Islands

Will you visit the Canary Islands? Risk 1.

The Cape of Fear. Throw again to pass.

Cape Bojador

Ships separated in a gale. Anchor at the Cape Verde Islands for 2 turns.

Cape Verde Islands

Ships together again. Move on one space.

You must decide whether to sail south-east or south-west. Throw again to move down the route of your choice.

Risk 2

Good winds. Move on one space.

Risk 3

Favourable currents. Move on one space.

Christmas Bay. Move on one space.

Risk 4

Winds against you. Miss a turn.

Risk 5

St. Helena Bay. Miss 2 turns to clean the ships.

Bad winds. Throw 2 tails in a row to leave this space.

Wait here for 3 turns while you break up the empty storeship and burn it.

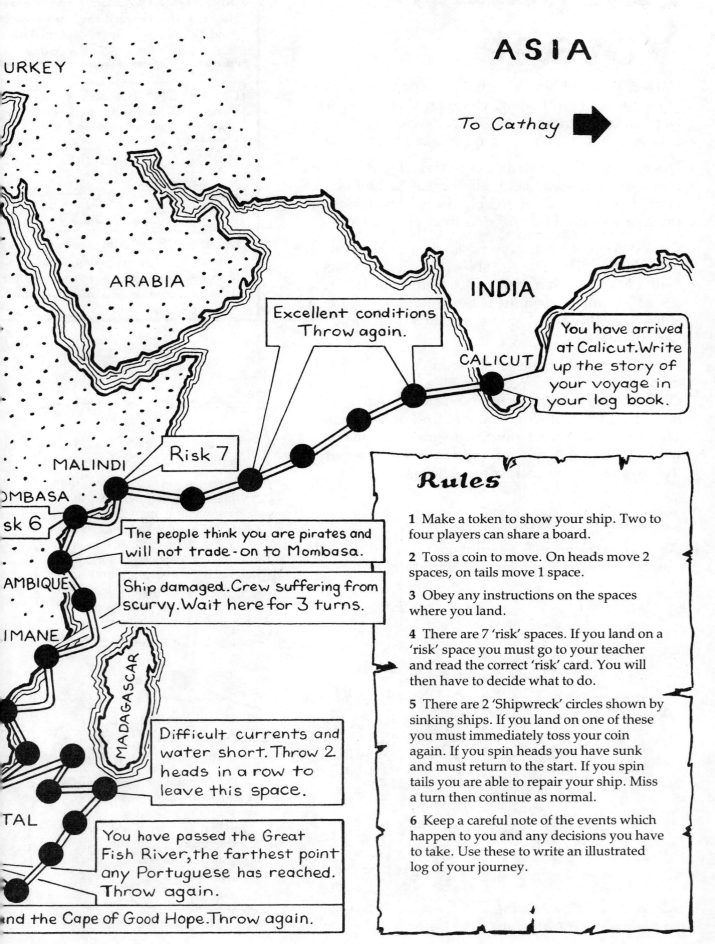

ASIA

To Cathay ➡

URKEY

ARABIA

INDIA

Excellent conditions
Throw again.

CALICUT

You have arrived at Calicut. Write up the story of your voyage in your log book.

Risk 7

MALINDI

OMBASA

sk 6

The people think you are pirates and will not trade - on to Mombasa.

AMBIQUE

Ship damaged. Crew suffering from scurvy. Wait here for 3 turns.

IMANE

MADAGASCAR

Difficult currents and water short. Throw 2 heads in a row to leave this space.

TAL

You have passed the Great Fish River, the farthest point any Portuguese has reached. Throw again.

nd the Cape of Good Hope. Throw again.

Rules

1 Make a token to show your ship. Two to four players can share a board.

2 Toss a coin to move. On heads move 2 spaces, on tails move 1 space.

3 Obey any instructions on the spaces where you land.

4 There are 7 'risk' spaces. If you land on a 'risk' space you must go to your teacher and read the correct 'risk' card. You will then have to decide what to do.

5 There are 2 'Shipwreck' circles shown by sinking ships. If you land on one of these you must immediately toss your coin again. If you spin heads you have sunk and must return to the start. If you spin tails you are able to repair your ship. Miss a turn then continue as normal.

6 Keep a careful note of the events which happen to you and any decisions you have to take. Use these to write an illustrated log of your journey.

A Spanish Voyage

In 1486, Christopher Columbus arrived at the court of Queen Isabella in Castile. His plan was to sail westwards to find a new route to Cipango and Cathay. He believed that the voyage would take about 30 days.

Queen Isabella turned Columbus down at first. However, she was eventually persuaded by her adviser, Luis de Santagel, to help. Isabella provided half the money Columbus needed to equip his ships.

On 3rd August 1492, Columbus' fleet sailed from the port of Palos. There were 3 ships. The flagship was the 'Santa Maria' with a crew of 40. Columbus described her as a 'dull sailer unfit for exploration'. The other ships were the 'Nina' with a crew of 30 and the 'Pinta' with a crew of 24.

There were no women or priests on board. The ships carried cheese, onions, vegetables, oil and vinegar. Daily rations for each sailor were a pound of ship's biscuits, 2 litres of wine and a pound of fish or meat. The ships also carried gunpowder and cannon balls as well as beads, mirrors, pins and needles. The story of the voyage is shown across these pages.

Columbus' return

On 15th March 1493 Columbus returned to Palos triumphantly. He was heaped with honours.

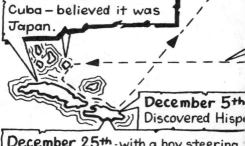

October 12th - the first sight of land. Juan Bermeo, a sailor on the 'Pinta', claimed the reward for first sighting land. Columbus kept it himself. The island was named San Salvador.

October 28th Discovered Cuba – believed it was Japan.

December 5th Discovered Hispe

December 25th - with a boy steering, 'Santa Maria' ran aground. The ship w unloaded. The timber was used to bu a fort manned by 43 officers and men from the ship.

Document A
Columbus describes the people of San Salvador

They go quite naked as their mothers bore them ... All that I saw were young men ... very well made, of very handsome bodies and good faces; the hair they wear over their brows except for a hank behind they wear long and never cut. Some of them paint themselves black, and some paint themselves white and others red ...

Document B
A description of the landing at San Salvador

... the Admiral went ashore in the armed ship's boat with the royal standard displayed ... having given thanks to Our Lord, kneeling on the ground ... the Admiral arose and gave the island the name San Salvador.

Columbus landing at San Salvador

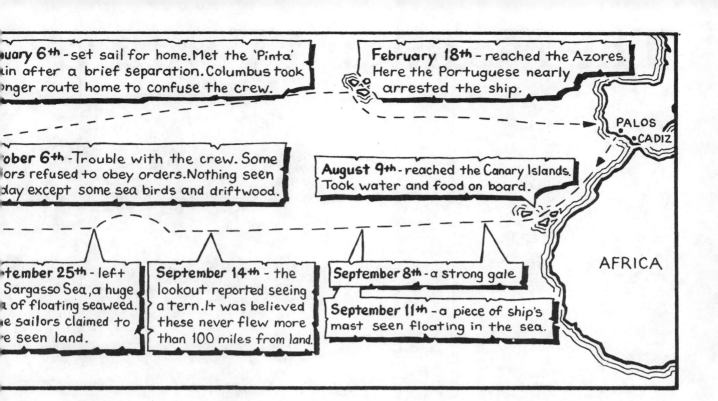

uary 6th - set sail for home. Met the 'Pinta' ...ain after a brief separation. Columbus took ...nger route home to confuse the crew.

February 18th - reached the Azores. Here the Portuguese nearly arrested the ship.

PALOS
CADIZ

...ober 6th - Trouble with the crew. Some ...ors refused to obey orders. Nothing seen ...day except some sea birds and driftwood.

August 9th - reached the Canary Islands. Took water and food on board.

AFRICA

...tember 25th - left ...Sargasso Sea, a huge ...a of floating seaweed. ...e sailors claimed to ...e seen land.

September 14th - the lookout reported seeing a tern. It was believed these never flew more than 100 miles from land.

September 8th - a strong gale

September 11th - a piece of ship's mast seen floating in the sea.

The 'Santa Maria'

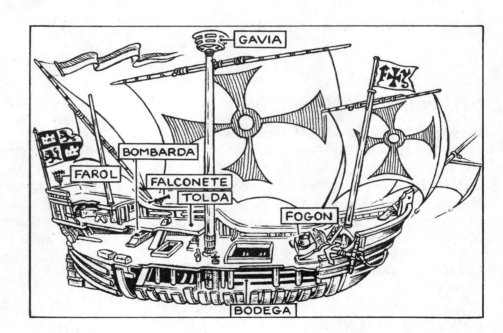

GAVIA
BOMBARDA
FAROL
FALCONETE
TOLDA
FOGON
BODEGA

1 Look at the picture of the 'Santa Maria'. Suggest English words for the following Spanish words:

Bombarda; bodega; fogon; falconette; gavia; tolda

2 Why would the farol (lantern) be very useful on this expedition?

3 How long did the voyage take?

4 Explain in your own words why Columbus took a longer route home.

5 Using the information on this page, write an imaginative illustrated diary of the voyage as if you were Columbus. Concentrate on your hopes and fears.

6 Write a speech to be made by Columbus to Queen Isabella, explaining the importance of his discoveries and what should be done next.

7 Look at the 2 documents and the picture of Columbus landing. Does Columbus' own description of the natives match the picture? What are the sailors at (A) doing? Does this match the description in Document B? Describe the behaviour of the Indians at (B) and (C). Use this and any other things you notice about the picture to answer these questions:
(i) Was the artist present at the landing? How do you know?
(ii) What impression of Columbus is the artist trying to give? Why?
(iii) Place the 2 documents and the picture in order of their importance to a historian. Give reasons for your choice.

The Mainland Venture

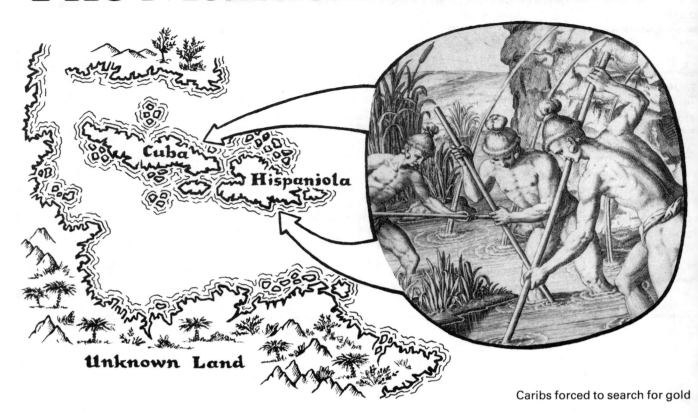

Caribs forced to search for gold

Settlement on Hispaniola

Between 1493 and 1504, Columbus made 3 more voyages to the New World. He searched desperately for a route to Cathay. He did not realise that he had discovered a new continent which blocked his path. Nor did he realise that Cathay lay thousands of miles further west across the Pacific Ocean.

Columbus started the first colony on Hispaniola (Haiti). He brought 1,200 people in 17 ships to live in the new settlement of Isabella. He also brought sugar cane which grew well on the islands.

There were many poor people in Spain who believed they could make their fortunes in the New World. They began to flood into the islands. They were given land to farm but this was not enough for them.

Many of the new settlers were very cruel. They forced the Indians (Caribs) to search for gold. Every Indian over the age of 14 had to bring in a hawk's bell full of gold dust every month. Many Indians were tortured and killed, and thousands more died from overwork and European diseases. Within 10 years nine-tenths of the Indians had been wiped out.

Life for the Spanish settlers was not easy either. Each was given an *encomienda* (grant of land) by Queen Isabella. This gave them 200 acres of land to farm provided they protected the Indians and converted them to the Christian faith. However, the soil was often poor and crops were hard to grow.

The latest news from the mainland

It is 1519. The explorer, Grijalva, has just returned from the mainland. He has reported finding a new country with strange and powerful Indians who

— spoke a completely new language
— gave the Spaniards a feast
— brought gold jewellery worth 16,000 pieces of eight and gave it to the Spaniards in exchange for a few beads
— wore cotton jackets, feather headdresses and carried wooden swords
— disappeared into the jungle leaving 2 prisoners who had been beheaded

Hernan Cortés was born in Spain in 1485. He was a soldier and gambler, who sailed to the New World to make his fortune. In 1511 he settled on the island of Cuba, where he was given a large estate. He married and became one of the most important people on the island. But he was determined to find more wealth. When he heard that Diego Velasquez, the Governor of Cuba, needed someone to lead an expedition to the mainland, Cortés sold his estate and bribed important officials in order to get the job.

He was of good height and body and well proportioned and robust ... in his eyes and expression there was something kindly yet grave ... He was a good horseman and skilful with all weapons on foot and on horseback and knew very well how to manage them. Above all he possessed courage and spirit which is what matters most of all. I have heard it said that when he was young ... he was somewhat dissolute about women and that he fought with knives several times with strong men and always won. He had a scar from a knife wound near his under-lip, and if one looked hard at it, he was inclined to cover it up more with his beard.

In all of which he showed ... signs of being a great lord ... He wore on his fingers a very rich ring with a diamond.

He dined well and he drank a good cup of wine and water which held a pint but he was not dainty nor did he care to eat of delicate and expensive dishes.

He recited prayers every morning ... and heard Mass with devoutness. When he was angry, a vein in his throat swelled up ... but he never said a foul or injurious word to any captain or soldier. He was very fond of cards and dice and was addicted to women in excess.

1 Read the description of Cortés.

2 List the points that made Cortés a good leader.

3 List the points that might have counted against Cortés as a leader.

4 Was Cortés fair and honest?

5 Was Cortés the ideal person to lead an expedition to the mainland?

6 Did the Spanish treat the Caribs fairly and honestly?

7 *Your decision*
You have been a farmer on Haiti for 9 years. You have an *encomienda* but the land is swampy and contains no gold. Cortés has asked you to join him on his expedition. You will have to supply your own weapons. He has promised a share of any gold he finds. Cortés is going to take 500 swordsmen, 32 crossbowmen, 13 musketeers, 100 sailors, 14 cannons, 16 horses and some dogs.
You can *either*
(a) Sell your estate, buy weapons and armour and join Cortés, *or*
(b) Carry on farming but try new crops.
Write a letter to Cortés explaining what decision you have made and why you have made it.

8 What do you think about the size and composition of this force?

9 Design a banner for the force to carry.

Aztec!

The Indians who had given the gold to Grijalva were known as the Aztecs. They were an Indian tribe who ruled a large Empire in Central America. The people of this Empire were members of many different tribes. The Aztecs had defeated them all in battle.

The Aztecs did not rule the people of the Empire directly. Instead they controlled them by collecting taxes or tribute. In the reign of Montezuma II, 371 cities paid tribute every 6 months to the Aztecs. A detailed tribute list was sent to every city in the Empire. The people had to send the goods immediately to the Aztec capital, Tenochtitlan. Any city which refused to send all the goods immediately was attacked by the Aztec army.

The Aztecs were a fighting people. Their own land was only good for growing maize and other basic crops. So they took the luxuries they needed, like cotton and gold, by fighting and conquest.

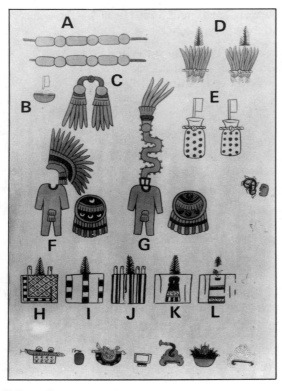

Tribute list

The powerful Aztec army defeated the neighbouring tribes. The most important soldiers were captured, and, along with hundreds of other families from the region, were sent to Tenochtitlan. These prisoners were sacrificed to the Aztec gods. In 1487, over 20,000 prisoners were sacrificed to celebrate the building of a new temple in Tenochtitlan. So Aztec raids kept other cities weak, and reminded them that tribute was less expensive than human lives.

Tribute

There were 3 main sorts of tribute sent to Tenochtitlan:

1 *Food.* The staple food in the Empire was maize (corn) which was ground into flour to make bread. The Aztecs demanded some maize as tribute although they were more interested in other foods. They particularly wanted fruits and vegetables from other areas, or luxury foods like meat and chocolate.

2 *Raw materials.* Some cities had their own gold mines. Some were near jungle areas where exotic birds were found. Their feathers were used to make colourful mosaics and headdresses. Some cities had emeralds or pearls which they had obtained by trading.

3 *Manufactured goods.* Most villages in the Empire made pottery items like plates and jugs. Women spun and wove cotton into richly decorated blankets or cloaks. Gold was used to make ornaments and everyday objects like plates. No tribe in Central America had discovered how to make things from iron. Weapons were made from wood and flint or obsidian (a hard stone).

This is a picture of a tribute list. It shows goods sent to Tenochtitlan from a number of villages. At the bottom of the page are the glyphs (picture words) for the villages which have given the goods.

An Aztec merchant shows his goods to the emperor

Cloaks made of cotton or feathers were the basic article of Aztec clothing. They were tied on one shoulder by a knot.

The Aztecs had no alphabet and used pictures for numbers. A feather stood for 400. A flag stood for 20. Fingers showed the numbers 1–10. The Aztec Treasurer had thousands of these tribute lists stored in a large house in Tenochtitlan.

As the Aztecs collected more goods as tribute, they began to trade with other more powerful countries. The Aztec merchants (*pochtea*) became very important. They would load up with huge quantities of trade goods, and set off for large markets and cities on the borders of the Empire.

All trade was based on barter (exchange) because the Aztecs had no coinage. The Aztecs did not use the wheel except as a toy. They also had no domestic animals or beasts of burden (horses, cattle etc.), so men and women were trained as porters to carry everything on their backs.

The merchants set out with 50 or 60 porters carrying goods. They were accompanied by Aztec soldiers who protected them on their long walk to market. At the market the merchants traded and returned home with gold, feathers, cotton, chocolate, rubber and live birds or animals for the Emperor's zoos.

1 List the goods brought back by the Aztec merchant in the picture above. How did he get these goods?

2 Look at the example of the tribute list. Write down what you think the items may be and how many of them there are. Explain why they would be valuable.

Merchants on the road

3 Using this example as a pattern, draw your own tribute list containing:
   2,400 loads of cloth cloaks
   5 suits of armour decorated with feathers
   4,000 loads of limes
   40 lion skins
   a chest of beans
   a chest of maize
   100 wood and flint axes
   20 bags of gold dust
   8,000 handfuls of scarlet feathers
   1,600 bundles of cotton.

4 Explain what tribute is and why it was important for the Aztecs.

5 Make a list of 6 things that could be bought cheaply in Europe (e.g. horseshoe, cartwheel) which the Aztecs had never seen.

6 Why did the Aztecs not trade with Europe?

7 Were the Aztecs rich and powerful? Give reasons for your answer.

Aztec Empire

Central America was settled by a number of Indian tribes. The Mayans built great temples and had an advanced system for law and government. The Mixtec tribe produced marvellous items in gold and pottery. The Toltec tribe built one great city around a temple.

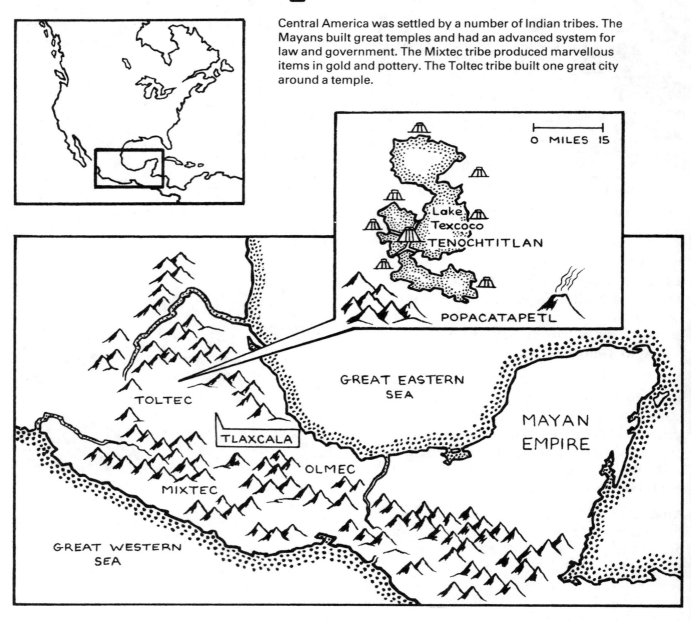

0 MILES 15

Lake Texcoco
TENOCHTITLAN
POPACATAPETL

TOLTEC

TLAXCALA

GREAT EASTERN SEA

MAYAN EMPIRE

OLMEC

MIXTEC

GREAT WESTERN SEA

Maize was the most important crop for all the Central American tribes. These pictures show maize being planted with a digging stick (1), the ground being hoed (2) and the cobs being harvested (3).

This *glyph* (picture writing) shows the Aztecs arriving at Lake Texcoco.
1 Draw the symbol used to show the Aztec homeland.
2 What are the figures carrying?
3 How is movement shown?

The Aztecs were a small, warlike tribe of Indians in the north of Mexico. In the late thirteenth century, they began to move south to find better lands for farming and settlement. They arrived on the shores of Lake Texcoco in 1325. One of their legends says that here the tribal elders saw the sign which their god (Huitzilopochtli) had told them to find. It was an eagle sitting on a cactus plant, eating a snake.

In fact, the site was not very promising. There were a few small islands near the lake shore, and some good soil around the edges of the lake, but the land could be flooded easily. As the lake was salty there was no fresh water. There were few good sites for houses, no natural crops and little shelter. But the site had one great advantage. By building their city in the lake, the Aztecs were very safe from their enemies, such as the Mixtec and Toltec Indians. These tribes had settled better areas, building cities and temples. The Aztecs built the first houses on the islands. They began to build floating gardens made of reeds and soil to create more farming land on the lake itself. Gradually the city

Thousands of these floating gardens (chinampas) surrounded the city of Tenochtitlan. How were they built? What were they used for?

expanded to become the Aztec capital, Tenochtitlan.

The Aztecs and all the other Indian tribes in Central America relied on maize as their main food crop. Maize was planted in shallow soil in the spring, using a planting stick. The seeds grew into tall plants during the summer. Then the corn was cut and stored.

Maize leaves and stalks were used to make baskets and to thatch roofs. The corn was ground into flour. The thin bread made from the corn—rather like a pancake—was called a *tortilla*. Tortillas could be filled with meat, fish or vegetables. Every Aztec meal included tortillas. Young children (under 8) were given 1 tortilla a day. Older children had 2. An adult would eat 3 a day.

1 Complete the table below to show how good the site the Aztecs had found on Lake Texcoco was. Give the site a mark out of 5 (5=excellent; 3=average; 1=poor) for each feature listed. Then write 2 or 3 sentences explaining the difficulties facing the early inhabitants on this site.

	MARK
Near to fresh water	
Safe from attacks	
Plenty of good farming land	
Not likely to flood	
Easy to build houses	
Not wanted by anyone else	

2 Draw pictures to show these 4 events in early Aztec history.
(a) The Aztecs wander across the desert looking for somewhere to settle.
(b) They arrive on the shores of Lake Texcoco.
(c) They build their first houses on the lake.
(d) They fight with a neighbouring group of Toltec Indians.

3 Describe the landscape and features of Mexico. One of the first Europeans to visit the country was asked to draw a map of Mexico. He crumpled up a piece of paper. Why?

4 The Aztecs soon began to spread out, fighting other tribes in the Valley of Mexico. List the advantages they could get by conquering these tribes.

Aztec Ruler

Montezuma

Montezuma became the Aztec ruler (He-who-speaks) in 1503. He was aged 34. He was the nephew of Ahuitzol, who ruled the Aztecs from 1486 to 1503 and grandson of Montezuma I, who ruled from 1440 to 1469.

At school (*calmelac*), Montezuma learned how to handle Aztec weapons (sling, sword and bow) and to read glyph writing. He could recite the history of the Aztec tribe and could interpret signs and omens. He was a skilful soldier and fought in many battles. He began his reign with a war, capturing many prisoners after a quick campaign in the southern part of the Empire.

As ruler he was the chief priest of the Aztecs, so he took part in the main ceremonies. One of these was the Great Fire ceremony. This was held every year to make sure that the world was not destroyed. Thousands of captives from rebel provinces were sacrificed.

Montezuma seems to have been a very good and popular ruler. The Aztecs collected tribute from more cities than ever before. All their enemies were defeated except for the Tlaxcala tribe, who won a famous victory against the Aztecs in 1515. Montezuma 'wept bitter tears' when he heard about this event. But he immediately began to reform his army, appointing new leaders.

He was advised by a council of 4 noblemen, but unlike other rulers he did not listen to all his civil servants. He mostly relied on advice from his courtiers, who were all noblemen (*caciques*). One writer said of him: 'Besides that he was a great justicier and very noble, he was very valiant and happy . . . and he obtained great victories and came to his greatness.'

One of the first Europeans to see Montezuma was a Spanish soldier, Bernal Diaz, who came to the land of the Aztecs in 1519.

Document A

When we came near to Mexico . . . the great Montezuma got down from his litter and these other great noblemen supported him beneath a marvellously rich canopy of green feathers, decorated with gold work, silver, pearls and green stones which hung from a sort of border . . . The great Montezuma was magnificently dressed, in their fashion, and wore sandals the soles of which are of gold and the upper parts decorated with precious stones . . . many more lords walked before the great Montezuma, sweeping the ground on which he was to tread, and laying down cloaks so that his feet should not touch the earth. Not one of these chieftains dared to look him in the face.

Fathers take their sons to school

The Aztec emperor giving food and clothing to his people

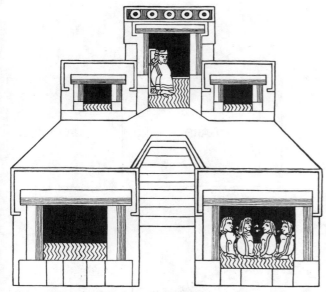

Montezuma and his council in his palace

1 The picture opposite shows Montezuma sitting in his palace in Tenochtitlan.
(a) Which person is Montezuma?
(b) Who are the other people?
(c) How do you know they are important people?
(d) Draw the Aztec glyphs for *Montezuma* and *speech*.
(e) What does this drawing tell you about the Aztec ruler?

Document B

The great Montezuma was about 40 years old, of good height, well proportioned, spare and slight, and not very dark, though of the usual Indian complexion. He was very neat and clean, and took a bath every afternoon. He had many women as his mistresses, the daughters of chieftains, but two legitimate wives who were caciques in their own right . . . He had a guard of 200 chieftains lodged in rooms besides his own, only some of whom were permitted to speak to him.

For each meal his servants prepared more than 30 dishes cooked in their native style . . . every day they cooked fowls, turkeys, pheasants, local partridges, quail, tame and wild duck, venison, wild boar, marsh birds, pigeons, hares and rabbits, also many kinds of birds and beasts native to their country.

His food was served on a long low table, covered with a white tablecloth. When he began his meal they placed in front of him a sort of wooden screen richly decorated with gold, so that no one should see him eat.

Test 1: Fight with a sword
A fight against 3 challengers using flint-tipped wooden swords. First to draw blood is the winner.

Test 2: Reading a star chart
Interpreting a picture of the heavens drawn by the Chief Priest. This will include recognising all the important stars and predicting what the harvest will be like.

Test 3: Fighting a mock battle
300 soldiers are sent into the countryside. The leader has to track them, surround them and capture them with a force of 500 soldiers.

2 The Aztec ruler was chosen from the royal family, but he did not have to be the son of the previous ruler. The young man most suitable for the job would be chosen by the Council of Four.

Look closely at the 3 tests above:
(a) Say how the tests might be helpful in choosing an Aztec leader.
(b) Which of the 3 tests is most important? Why?
(c) What was the most important job for the Aztec leader?

3 (Use both documents to help you.)
(a) What evidence is there that Montezuma was very important?
(b) Choose the 3 best examples which show how rich he was. Choose the 3 best examples which show how powerful he was.
(c) Describe the food, clothes and entertainment of the Aztec leader.
(d) What did Diaz think of Montezuma?
(e) Why did the Aztecs obey Montezuma?

4 Compare Montezuma with a European ruler of this time. You could choose Elizabeth I of England (see pages 48 and 49 of this book). Who would you say was the more powerful, and why?

Aztec City

A ROAD	A HOUSE	A TEMPLE	A GARDEN	HUMAN SKULL

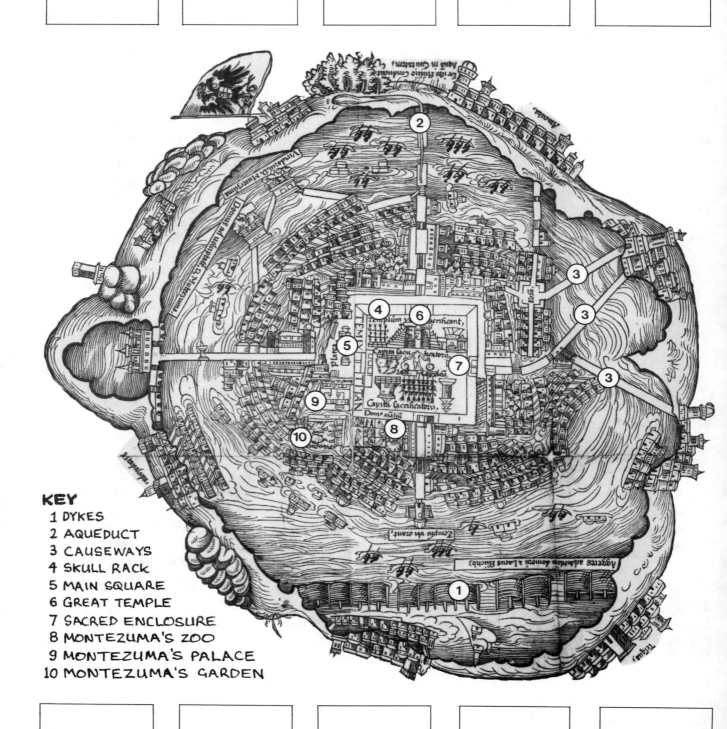

KEY
1 DYKES
2 AQUEDUCT
3 CAUSEWAYS
4 SKULL RACK
5 MAIN SQUARE
6 GREAT TEMPLE
7 SACRED ENCLOSURE
8 MONTEZUMA'S ZOO
9 MONTEZUMA'S PALACE
10 MONTEZUMA'S GARDEN

A PRIEST'S KNIFE	MONTEZUMA'S HEADDRESS	A CANDLE	PROTECTION AGAINST FLOODS	WILD ANIMAL

The main city of the Aztec Empire was Tenochtitlan. The city was an island. The first settlers had built their houses on 2 small islands in the middle of the lake. Gradually the surrounding lake was filled in and gardens were built on rafts of reeds. By 1500 the city was 1¾ miles square, covering an area of 2,500 acres, and containing at least 90,000 people. This made it the largest city in the world at this time. London, for example, had only 40,000 people.

The Aztecs reached the city by several wide causeways (roads). Each one was guarded by a fort. These protected the city. Travellers and traders had to pay to use the causeways.

The rich people had houses made of brick and stone, which were raised on stone platforms. The poorer people made their houses from mud, with thatched roofs. Most houses were one storey high and brilliantly coloured. Most houses had gardens.

Many of the 'roads' in the city were canals. So there was much canoe traffic.

In the centre of the city was a huge square. It contained many magnificent temples and the palace of Montezuma. Since the city was a great trading centre there was also a huge market. The Spaniards were amazed at its size.

Over 2,000 traders sold goods from shops and stalls. In one week as many as 50,000 customers passed through the market. This is how a modern historian described the scene:

This was a great square as large as a town. Each trader had his own area, which had to be kept clean and neat. Bernal Diaz wrote that in one place there would be gold, silver and jewels for sale, along with imported stones and feathers; in the next row, lines of slaves, in the next area varieties of cloth. Other goods on sale included maize, turkeys, dogs, honey and salt in the food shops; vases, plates and statues in the pottery shops; firewood, bamboo pipes, matting, stoves. Cortés wrote: 'In the market place there are places like apothecaries' shops where they sell medicines ready to be taken, ointments and poultices. There are barbers' shops, where one can be washed and trimmed; there are houses where, upon payment, one may eat or drink.'

Fresh water was brought to the city by 2 large stone aqueducts. Careful arrangements were made for the disposal of sewage. Public lavatories were built and 1,000 people were employed every day to clean up the city. The streets were swept and sprinkled with water. Waste was loaded into barges and carried away to be used as fertiliser. Dykes were built to protect the houses from flooding.

There was little crime in Tenochtitlan. There was no record of any plague. It was a well run, busy and wealthy city. Diaz commented: 'Among us were soldiers who had been in many parts of the world, at Constantinople, all over Italy, at Rome: and they said they had never seen a market so well ordered, so large and so crowded with people.'

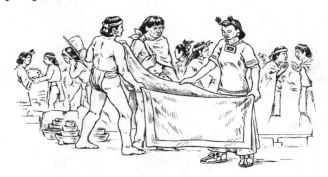

1 Describe the arrangements made in the city for each of the following:
(a) Getting a supply of fresh water
(b) Protecting the city from floods
(c) Worship
(d) Defence

2 Give your own opinion on each of the following, explaining your answer in each case.
(a) Was Tenochtitlan a well planned and healthy city?
(b) Would Tenochtitlan be easy to attack?
(c) Does the city show that the Aztecs were an advanced civilisation?

3 What evidence can you find on these pages that the Aztecs practised human sacrifice?

4 Compare Tenochtitlan with a European city in the sixteenth century. You will find some information to help you on page 46 onwards in this book, but you might like to use the library as well. You should mention buildings, planning, transport, sanitation and comfort.

5 Draw a simple plan of Tenochtitlan in your book.

6 Copy the squares at the top and bottom of the map. In them draw a suitable picture (glyph) instead of the words.

7 Draw arrows from the boxes into the city to show where you would be likely to find each object.

Aztec Beliefs

The god of learning and crafts. Helped people to learn how to weave cloth and make pottery, feather and corn items—such as lamps and rope.

The god of the sky. Made the wind blow at the right time, controlled day, night and the weather.

The god of rain. Made rain fall at the right time, which helped all the crops to grow.

The god of war. The personal god of the Aztecs, who had guided them to Tenochtitlan and led them in every battle.

The Aztecs believed that gods made the earth and controlled all the people. The most important possession of an Aztec family was its own land and crops. So the most important Aztec gods were those who controlled the natural forces such as the wind, rain and sun. These gods had most effect on ordinary Aztec life. The Aztec name for the sun was Ihalnemohuani ('He by whom people live').

Four of the most important Aztec gods are shown in the drawings above. The Aztecs prayed to over 300 gods and goddesses, each with his or her own name and special responsibility.

Priests and priestesses were very important in Aztec society. They made the calendars and kept time. This gave them great power, since they alone knew the best time to perform special ceremonies. They also learned to foretell the future. They claimed to be able to do this because they could talk to the gods.

They also looked after the great temples in Tenochtitlan and other cities. Here they carried out all the ceremonies and sacrifices.

Their lives were not easy. They were not allowed to marry. They had to follow a very strict daily routine, praying at the temple 4 times a day, and 5 times at night. They used to give small amounts of their own blood to the sun god to feed him in his struggle against darkness (see picture). Without this blood they believed the sun would not rise.

The Aztecs believed in magic. The number 20 was a magic number because it was the number of fingers and toes a person had. There were 20 named days in the Aztec calendar. Each day had its own god. On these days miracles could happen if the god was pleased.

There were 18 months in the Aztec year, each with 20 days. Each month had a number of ceremonies, such as the sacrifice to the fire god in the ninth month. There were 5 unmarked days at the end of the year ($18 \times 20 = 360$) and these were a time of bad luck.

Aztec priests giving their own blood to the sun god

30

The Aztecs believed that the gods could be made happy if they were given presents. The greatest gift that the gods could give to humans was life itself. So life was the greatest offering that humans could give back to the gods.

Thousands of prisoners and slaves were killed every year as human sacrifices on the temple altars. Their hearts were cut out by a sharp stone knife and offered to the gods. If they died bravely and quickly the gods were pleased.

● Complete this calendar to show all 20 named days. Use only glyphs (picture writing). The calendar picture will help you.

A calendar stone showing the history of the world. It is over 4 metres in diameter.

DAY	1 Monkey	2 Grass	3 Reed	4 Ocelot	5 Eagle
GOD OF	*Flowers*	*Medicine*	*A demon*	*Earth*	*Seedtime*
DAY	6 Vulture	7 Motion	8 Flint knife	9 Rain	10 Flower
GOD OF	*Stars*	*A monster*	*Death*	*Home*	*Flowers*
DAY	11 Crocodile	12 Wind	13 House	14 Lizard	15 Serpent
GOD OF	*Creating*	*Learning*	*Mountains*	*Tricks*	*Water*
DAY	16 Death's head	17 Deer	18 Rabbit	19 Water	20 Dog
GOD OF	*Moon*	*Rain*	*Drink*	*Fire*	*Death*

The table shows the number of the day, the glyph and the god of that day.

See Teachers' Notes, page T5.

1 Explain how each of the 4 gods shown might help an ordinary Aztec family to grow and use its crop of maize.

2 Choose a suitable gift for each of the 4 gods.

3 If you were an Aztec priest, how might you explain the following?
(a) A farmer's field is ruined. The earth dries up, hardens and cracks. The field sinks.
(b) A man marries a young girl but refuses to join in the wedding feast. Within a week he is dead.

(c) The son of your best friend is chosen as a sacrifice to the sun. He lives in splendour and luxury for a year. He will be sacrificed tomorrow.

4 As an Aztec priest, suggest the best days on which to hold the following:
(a) a ceremony to cure the ruler of a fever
(b) a ceremony to help the crops grow
(c) a ceremony to display Aztec gold and treasure.
Describe what would happen at each ceremony.

Aztec Warfare

Holtec wears the headdress of a Jaguar Knight. This shows that he is a very rich and important warrior. There are 2 other orders of Knights—the Eagle Knights and the Arrow Knights. Each knight leads a squadron of 200 or more soldiers in the army.

Holtec's shield is made of wood and decorated with feathers. It can stop arrows and is useful against stones, clubs and other weapons.

HOLTEC
A Jaguar Knight

Holtec wears body armour made of quilted cotton soaked in salt water. It is dyed to make it look like a jaguar skin. The armour is very tough and cannot easily be pierced by spears or arrows. All knights wear body armour. The other soldiers wear war paint and feathers. Most soldiers are villagers, called to fight at times of emergency.

Holtec's main aim in fighting is to capture prisoners. These are sent to Tenochtitlan for sacrifice. Any warrior who captures 4 prisoners is given a reward of land, and can become a knight. Aztec judges and other important officials are chosen from the knights.

Holtec's main weapon is a broadsword made of wood and edged with pieces of obsidian (hard stone). It is so sharp that it can cut off a horse's head with one blow. You can see this better below. Other weapons which he uses are a javelin, tipped with 2 or 3 obsidian barbs; and a sling which throws small stones. Other soldiers in his squadron use clubs and bows. The arrows are tipped with bone.

The man on the left is tied to a heavy stone which is richly carved. The knight is in full armour. What do you think may be happening here?

The Tolmacs

It is the year One-Rabbit. The city of Tolmac is about 500 km from Tenochtitlan. Its people are fierce and independent, with their own chief and gods. They have only a small army but all the citizens will fight bravely. They know about the Aztecs, but are not part of the Empire. Tolmac is a rich and important city.

Two Aztec chiefs arrived at Tolmac 20 days ago bringing a present for the city—some cheap mats made of corn stalks. The chiefs said they wanted the Tolmacs and the Aztecs to be friends. The mats are a token of their friendship.

They have given the Tolmacs 20 days to reply by sending a gift to Tenochtitlan. The only gift that will satisfy them is land.

The Aztecs have an army of nearly 100,000 men. Like the tribal armies, it is trained in fierce hand-to-hand fighting.

The Indians on the right of the picture are in the Tolmac army.
- Would you give in to the Aztec demands if you were a Tolmac? Explain.

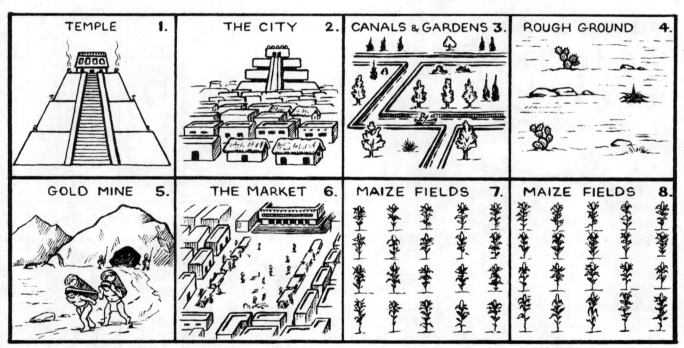

The picture shows the city and territory of the Tolmacs. It is divided into 8 marked squares, each with some special feature.

You are the Aztec commander. You have a large, well-trained and experienced army of knights and soldiers. It is divided into 3 sections—the Jaguars, the Eagles and the Arrows. Each section has 4,000 foot-soldiers and 1,000 knights.

1 Here is the battle plan a real Aztec commander would have followed. Discuss each move with other members of your group then explain what

its purpose was:
(a) Send greetings and weapons to the Tolmacs.
(b) Ambush and capture as many Tolmacs as possible.
(c) Surround the city and advance at a signal, displaying weapons and shouting.

2 Why will you beat the Tolmacs?

3 You capture the city. What are you going to do with (a) the temple, (b) the people?

4 Why do you leave the maize fields and the city unharmed?

5 Why will the Tolmacs never threaten you again?

33

Aztec Village

START

PLANTING MAIZE

There is light rain and sun for a month

There is no rain at all for two months

All the maize seeds grow well

There is a great wind. Many maize plants are blown down

Your clan is give[n] more land and [?] plants more ma[ize]

The ground dr[ies] up and crack[s]

END. You are sacrificed. Your heart is offered to the Sun God.

FARM[ING]

Stay single	Stick a thorn in your arm	Give away all your money	Learn the calendar	Preach peace	Learn to read
6	5	4	3	2	1

Learn to play the drums	Learn to ride a horse	Make a feather head-dress	Learn to read	Learn to use a bow	Learn to scalp
6	5	4	3	2	1

Grow maize	Buy building stone	Buy a load of feathers	Learn to read	Learn to count	Buy a ship
6	5	4	3	2	1

FIGH[T]

100 VILLAGERS are sent to TENOCHTITLAN to please the FIRE GOD

END

VILLAGE FESTIVAL

A fire destroys many houses

Your village gains land and treasure from another clan

All the slaves are sacrificed

100 slaves are sent to your village

The maize is not planted

One of your clan is made an Eagle Knight

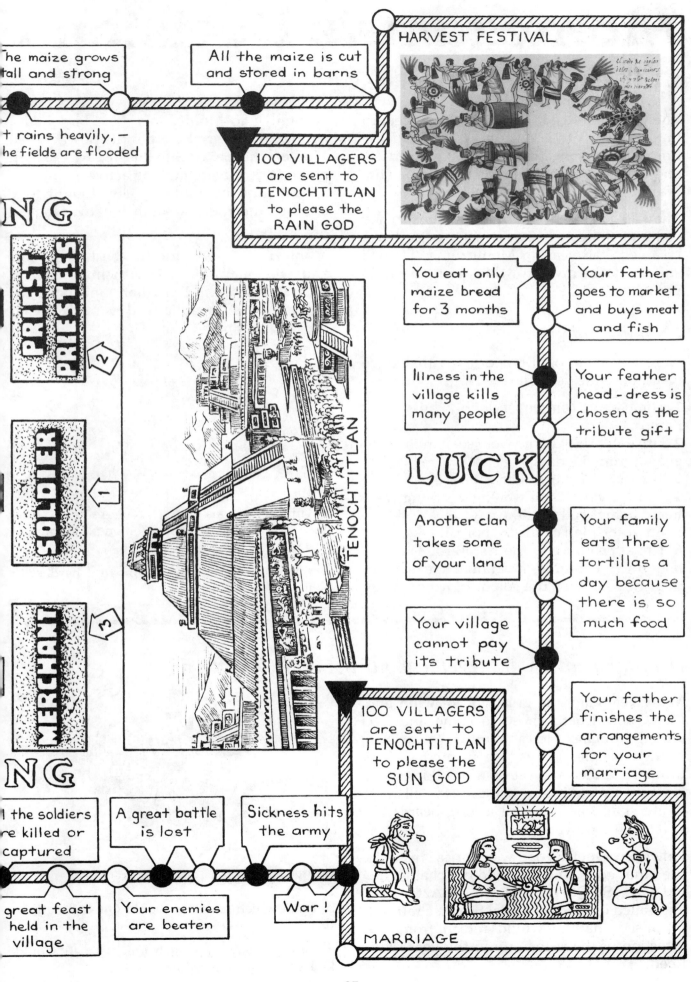

Montezuma's Decision 1

STAGE 1: The Year One-Reed

The year One-Reed (1519) is the seventeenth in the reign of Montezuma. As usual the Emperor has called together his chief priests and advisers to make predictions about the year.

They look at the signs and omens. They come to the conclusion that One-Reed will be a very bad year for Montezuma: 'He will suffer a great mystery which must come to pass in his land.'

Omens and signs

Here are some of the bad signs that have come since the year Twelve-House:

1 The Great Temple suddenly burst into flames.
2 Fire and bright lights were seen in the sky, even during the day.
3 The city of Tenochtitlan was flooded.
4 Strange voices and wailing or crying were heard at night all over the city.
5 A two-headed child was born.
6 The appearance of the Ash Bird. The lake fishermen captured a strange creature in their nets—a bird the colour of ashes. They

brought it to Montezuma. The bird had a strange mirror in the top of its head. When Montezuma looked into this he saw a distant plain. People were moving across it quickly, spread out in ranks. They fought one another and rode on animals which looked like deer.

Montezuma called for his best magicians and wise men. He asked them to explain what he had seen. But when they looked in the mirror everything had vanished, and they saw nothing.

1 This picture was drawn by the Aztecs to show one of these omens. Which omen is the picture describing?

2 Which of the omens do you find hardest to believe? Why?

An important Aztec legend about the year One-Reed

Many years ago the great god of wind and life, Quetzalcoatl, chose to come and live among humans. He came down to earth to change people's ways. He wanted to end human sacrifice and set up a new kingdom. He was a magnificent being, very tall with white skin, fair hair and a long beard. He had magical powers.

However, Quetzalcoatl was not as strong as the other gods, and he could not change the old ways. So Quetzalcoatl left the Aztec land and sailed off into the Great Sea on a raft. He promised that he would return from the direction of the rising sun in the year One-Reed.

Quetzalcoatl

3 From which direction would Quetzalcoatl return?

4 List the ways in which Quetzalcoatl would look different from ordinary Aztecs.

STAGE 2: News from the Great Sea in the direction of the rising sun

Soon after the predictions about the year One-Reed, Montezuma hears news that strangers have arrived in his kingdom. They come from the direction of the rising sun.

A man from the coast reports seeing strangers. He says that they came from mountains floating on the sea.

Montezuma receives other reports about the strangers. He is told that they have long beards and fair hair.

Montezuma orders his craftsmen to make an exact copy of the clothes worn only by Quetzalcoatl. He sends messengers to find out more about the strangers. This is the report they made when they returned to Montezuma.

Look at this Aztec picture of this event:

1 What were the mountains which the man from the coast spoke about? Why did he call them mountains?

The report of Montezuma's messengers

'We carried the clothes and many other valuable presents. We were taken onto the strangers' ship and presented the costume to their leader. He put it on. The leader then asked if these were all the gifts we had brought.

When this had been done a great thing was fired off. A thing like a ball of stone came out of its entrails (inside). It came out shooting sparks and raining fire. The smoke that came out of it had an evil smell like rotten mud. They aimed this thing at a mountain. The mountain split and cracked open. It was aimed at a tree. It shattered the tree into splinters.

The strangers dress in iron. Their swords are iron; their bows are iron; their shields are iron; their spears are iron. Their deer carry them on their backs wherever they wish to go. These deer, our Lord, are tall as the roof of a house.

The strangers' bodies are completely covered, so that only their faces can be seen. Their skin is white as if they were made of lime. They have long yellow hair, although some of them have black. Their beards are long and yellow and their hair is curly.'

When Montezuma hears this report he is filled with terror. It is as if his heart has fainted, as if it has shrivelled. He seems conquered by despair.

Montezuma, terrified, thinks about hiding

2 Who did Montezuma think the strangers might be? What evidence did he have for this idea?

3 Why was Montezuma so terrified by the news his messengers brought?

4 Look at the document. What is the object which fires 'a ball of stone from its entrails'? Why were the messengers so impressed by the strangers?

5 The costume given to the strangers was the feathered cloak of the great god Quetzalcoatl. Did the strangers pass or fail the 'test of the cloak' of Quetzalcoatl? Explain.

6 Did Montezuma's messengers tell him the truth about everything they saw? Explain your answer.

Montezuma's Decision 2

STAGE 3: Advising Montezuma

Montezuma is now faced with a terrible problem. Are the strangers Quetzalcoatl and his followers, who have returned as the legends predicted? If so they may bring peace and plenty, or they may destroy the Empire and Montezuma's power. Are the strangers just bandits out for as much loot as they can get? Are they the advance guard of an invasion? Do they have magical powers, or are they just human? The future of the Aztec Empire rests in Montezuma's hands. If he chooses wrongly his Empire may be destroyed.

For several years Montezuma has been brooding over the legend. He has lost interest in ruling his people and no longer controls the army. He has surrounded himself with magicians and priests. He asks them for interpretations of the omens, and hopes to find some way to win the favour of the gods.

PLAN 1 *Invite the strangers to the Aztec capital Tenochtitlan*

Advantages
Montezuma can see the strangers for himself and decide who they are. He can murder them if they prove to be bandits. If they are gods, he can impress them by showing his loyalty.

Disadvantages
If they are enemies Montezuma will have invited them to the centre of his Empire. They will be in the best place to take it over. They can easily kill Montezuma and loot the capital.

PLAN 2 *Warn the strangers not to come any nearer the capital*

Advantages
This may keep the strangers away from the centre of the Empire. If they keep away, they will not be in such a good position to threaten Montezuma and the Empire.

Disadvantages
If the strangers are bandits they may suspect that Montezuma is afraid of them. This may encourage them to be more aggressive and threatening. If they are gods, they will be angry.

PLAN 3 *Send impressive gifts to the strangers*

Advantages
If they are gods, they will be impressed with the magnificent gifts. If they are bandits, this may satisfy their greed.

Disadvantages
If they are gods, they may not be impressed. They may prefer human hearts as gifts. If they are bandits, the gifts will show them how rich the Aztecs are, and make them greedy for more.

1 *EITHER*

(a) You are the Royal Astrologer. Prepare an illustrated astrological prediction for the year One-Reed, using what you have learned from Stages 1 and 2. This will be given to Montezuma and it should contain pictures and information on

    the omens
    legends
    the strangers
    what will happen.

OR

(b) You are a Jaguar Knight who does not believe the strangers are Quetzalcoatl and his followers. Prepare and make a speech to Montezuma that explains the omens, the legends, the strangers, their equipment and their actions.

2 Which do you think Montezuma is most likely to believe and why?

Below are 6 plans which Montezuma is considering. Read each one carefully, then answer the questions at the end.

3 Which plans do you think each of the following 2 people at Montezuma's court might have advised the ruler to follow? Choose 2 plans for each person. Give reasons for your answers.

(a) The Royal Astrologer. He is very religious.

He is certain that the strangers are gods.

(b) The Jaguar Knight. He is a brave soldier who likes fighting. He does not believe the rumours about the strangers being gods. He knows how to deal with bandits.

4 What new plan might be put forward by the Chief Priest or Priestess of Montezuma's court, who knows that the gods will be made happy by human sacrifices?

5 If you were Montezuma, which 2 plans would you choose and why?

6 Montezuma chose Plans 2 and 3. Why do you think he chose these?

7 Why do you think that Plans 2 and 3 have been described by one historian as the worst possible choices Montezuma could have made?

PLAN 4   *Send an army to attack the strangers*

Advantages
The army is 100,000 strong. It may destroy the strangers, which will get rid of the problem for ever.

Disadvantages
If the strangers have magical weapons, the army may be defeated. This may mean the end of the Aztecs.

PLAN 5   *Set impossible tasks which will prove whether the strangers are gods*

Advantages
This will show whether the strangers really are gods. If they fail the tests, it will prove they are just bandits.

Disadvantages
Real gods will be very angry at being doubted in this way.

PLAN 6   *Do nothing but wait to see what happens*

Advantages
This will cost nothing, and no lives will be lost. The strangers will eventually show beyond all doubt whether they are gods or humans. If they are gods, Montezuma will have done nothing to anger them. If they are human, they may die of disease or just go away.

Disadvantages
The strangers and the rebellious cities in the Empire may take this as a sign of Montezuma's weakness, and join together against the Aztecs. If they are gods, they will be angry at not being greeted with the proper respect.

Conquest

Cortés' expedition left Cuba in 1519. The Spanish landed and fought a battle with the people of the city of Tabasco. The Spanish won easily. They were given rich presents. In the city they met an Indian Princess called Marina who joined the expedition, acting as interpreter for Cortés.

Travelling further along the coast the Spanish met a small group of important officials from Tenochtitlan. They presented Cortés with jewels and a gold plate. The more presents he received, the more determined Cortés was to continue to the capital. The Aztecs were impressed by the Spanish calling them lords and gods.

Cortés then destroyed the ships so the Spanish could not retreat, and moved inland to the city of Tlaxcala. The Tlaxcalans attacked but the Spanish won another easy victory. The Tlaxcalans hated the Aztecs and saw a chance to destroy them by joining the powerful strangers. They provided 1,000 porters and a large army for Cortés.

The following section is the story of Cortés' first visit to Tenochtitlan as a Spanish soldier might have described it. The pictures were drawn by Aztecs.

After many weeks of walking through freezing mountains, we arrived on the shores of the lake which holds the Aztec city. We were amazed at its size. Some of the buildings were huge. We marvelled at the great causeways. Some of us who had seen cities like Venice or Constantinople thought that this was far more magnificent.

1 Spanish soldier

Suddenly trumpets sounded and a procession came out from the city. It was the Aztec leader, Montezuma, and his royal guards. Montezuma greeted us as friends. Marina told us that he said 'You have come back to us. You have come down from the sky. Rest now and take possession of your royal houses. Welcome to your land, my lords.' Cortés replied, 'Tell Montezuma that we are his friends. There is nothing to fear.' We were then allowed to enter the city, and were housed in a great palace in the main square.

We stayed in the palace for a week or two. We were well treated, but we had not come all this way and fought so

2 Cortés in Tlaxcala

1 Look carefully at picture 2. Who is the person seated? Who is the person standing on his left? Who are the 3 people standing in a group? What are they doing? What are the objects on the floor?

2 Describe the weapons used by the Aztecs.

3 What other objects do the Aztecs carry into battle? What are they for?

4 What evidence can you find in the pictures that Cortés had Indian allies?

5 Using the pictures describe the Spanish weapons. In what 2 important ways are they different from Aztec weapons?

6 Why do you think the Aztecs wanted to sacrifice the Spanish?

hard to be treated like lap-dogs. We were all anxious for action. We were made impatient by the sight of luxury and riches around us. The sight of the daily sacrifice of victims at the great temple hardened the heart of our leader, who decided that the city should be taken.

'It will give me great pleasure,' he said, 'to fight for my God against your gods, who are a mere nothing.' And fight we did.

The captain's plan was simple. We held Montezuma captive in our palace and made him order his people not to fight. Cortés left to meet a new army coming from Cuba. Those of us remaining became nervous and angry. We decided to attack the temple and destroy the blood-sucking priests.

3 Attack on the temple

The whole city rose up against us. A great crowd formed in front of our palace, yelling and shouting. We pushed Montezuma out onto the balcony, hoping that he would calm the riot. But the people called out the name Cuitlahac and threw stones and sticks onto the balcony. Marina told us that they had chosen Cuitlahac as their new leader. Montezuma was killed by the stones thrown by his own people.

When our captain returned he had to fight his way into the city. He realised that we were hopelessly outnumbered, and that if we stayed in the city we would be massacred. He ordered us to gather our equipment and leave. We made a wooden bridge so that we could cross any gaps that might have been made in the causeway. When it was dark we moved out of the city.

4 Rising in the city

The Aztecs raised the alarm and within minutes we were surrounded. I thought my hour had come. A hail of stones and arrows rained down. But they did not press home their attack. Instead they sent raiding parties who seized some of our men and took them back to the temple. We heard later that they were sacrificed.

The rest of us forced our way along the western causeway, fighting inch by inch in the dark until we escaped the accursed city. Over half our number had been captured or killed. Most of the rest of us were wounded. I had an arrow wound in my thigh. The captain took one last look at the city, and promised to return. Then he led us back to Tlaxcala and safety.

5 Fighting in the city

7 Why was Princess Marina so important to Cortés?

8 Think of reasons why both the story and the pictures may not be a completely accurate account of these events.

9 Write the story as if you were an Aztec. You should think about the following:

The arrival of the gods; Montezuma's warm welcome; kind treatment for the strangers; special sacrifices made for them; the departure of Quetzalcoatl; the treachery of the remaining strangers; the treachery of Montezuma; the battle to stop the strangers leaving the city. You could do some pictures of your own to illustrate the story.

The End of the Empire

Cortés spent 10 months assembling a new force that would be able to defeat the Aztec army and capture the city of Tenochtitlan.

What Cortés knew about Tenochtitlan:

1 The Aztec capital relied on the 2 aqueducts for fresh water.

2 Most of the food for the city came from the towns in the Empire.

3 The Tlaxcalans promised to provide thousands of trained soldiers, so that Cortés could lead a very large army against the city.

4 The Aztecs could not fight against cavalry.

5 Aztec armour was useless against cannon-fire and gun-shots.

6 No Indian tribes liked the Aztecs. Few would help them.

7 The Aztecs were determined fighters who would surrender only if they were outnumbered. By this stage they looked on the Spaniards as their enemies and not their friends.

8 The city was surrounded by water. It could only be approached across the causeways. These would be easy for the Aztecs to defend.

9 There were reports coming out of Tenochtitlan that thousands of Aztecs were dying from smallpox. They had no defence against this European disease. A disaster like this would shake their confidence and ruin the organisation of the army.

Spanish supplies and weapons

ITEM	PICTURE	HOW IT MIGHT BE USED
Boats		Surround the island-city, stop any supplies getting through
Horses		
Arquebuses		
Crossbows		
Cannons		
Tlaxcalans		
Spanish soldiers		

The final attack on Tenochtitlan

Cortés used his ships to bombard the city with cannons. They also kept away the canoes which tried to reach Tenochtitlan.

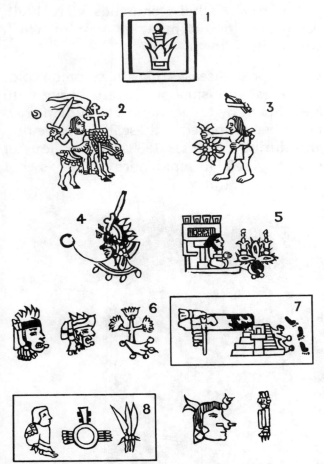

1 = One-Reed; 2 = strangers; 3 = friendly Aztecs; 4 = Montezuma; 5 = bad omens; 6 = events in Tenochtitlan; 7 = destruction of the temple; 8 = defeat and surrender

1 Look carefully at the list of Spanish weapons and supplies sent from Cuba. Copy the table into your book. Complete it by writing a sentence in the last column to show how you would advise Cortés to use each item against Tenochtitlan.

2 Prepare a detailed plan for Cortés. Explain how he should set about capturing the city of Tenochtitlan.

3 The picture opposite shows the Aztec story of what happened in the years One-Reed and Two-Knife. Write 2 or 3 sentences explaining what the picture is saying. Design your own Aztec picture to show the events of the conquest.

4 Compare the weapons of a Spanish and an Aztec soldier. Write a description of an arquebus and a crossbow as if you were an Aztec. Explain why you are afraid of them.

5 After 75 days Tenochtitlan surrendered. This was the end of the Aztec Empire. Explain the part played in the defeat of the Aztecs by each of the following: (a) the Tlaxcalans; (b) Cortés; (c) smallpox.

6 Why did the Empire fall? Write a letter from a Spanish priest to explain why the Aztecs were defeated. How might an Aztec priest have explained the end of the Empire?

New Spain

In 1522 Cortés was appointed Governor and Captain-General of New Spain, the lands previously ruled by the Aztecs. Within a few years the Spaniards also controlled Guatemala and Honduras.

New Spain was to be a model colony. Cattle, plants and ploughs were sent from Europe. Hundreds of Catholic priests were sent out and new churches were built. Many new cities were planned.

Most of Tenochtitlan had been destroyed in 1522. In its place, Mexico City was built as the capital of New Spain. A new cathedral was built on the site of the great temple in the main square. Montezuma's treasure houses and zoo were pulled down.

In the beginning vast amounts of treasure were sent back to Spain. But once New Spain had been looted, it was a disappointment. The gold mines produced very little. The land grew hardly any crops that could be sold in Europe. Although Cortés sent out 4 expeditions to look for spices, none were found.

In 1528, Cortés was replaced as governor of New Spain by the Viceroy, Antonio de Mendoza. Cortés returned to Spain in 1540 to complain to the king. He was kept waiting for years. One letter he wrote to the king was not answered for 3 years. A minor official had written 'no need to reply' on the back. Cortés died aged 63, an unhappy, bitter man.

What happened to the Aztecs?

The Aztec Empire and system of government disappeared, as all the Indians were forced to become subjects of the king of Spain.

A There were no more Aztec rulers after Cuitlahac. New Spain was ruled by a Spanish Viceroy.

B Indians were no longer allowed to own any land, even though they were supposed to be free to grow their own crops. The Spanish settlers made them work so hard that they had no time of their own.

C Many Indians were forced to work in the mines or on building sites. They were usually treated very harshly.

D The Aztec religion was outlawed. All the people of New Spain had to become Catholics. Anyone who refused could be killed. There were no more Aztec ceremonies. Over 12,000 new Catholic churches were built, using the stone from Aztec temples which were pulled down.

E European diseases, like the common cold, influenza and smallpox, were brought to New Spain by the settlers. The Indians had never been exposed to these illnesses before, and during the years 1530–1600 millions of Indians died in epidemics which swept across the country.

1 Indians working in New Spain

2 Aztecs being mistreated

1 Use the plan of the city of Tolmac on page 33 to do this exercise.
You are a Spanish official appointed by the Viceroy of New Spain. Your task is to reorganise the city of Tolmac. Explain what you will do about each square.
Your main aims are:
(a) to destroy Aztec power,
(b) to produce more European crops like wheat,
(c) to send as much gold as you can to Spain,
(d) to convert the people to the Catholic faith.
Explain what arrangements you intend to make for the people of Tolmac—the army, the slaves, the priests and the citizens.

2 List the different jobs being done by the Indians in pictures 1 and 2.

3 Give 3 examples of cruelty to Indians in picture 2.

4 Do you think picture 2 was drawn by a Spanish settler or an Indian? Give your reasons.

5 What is the artist trying to say about the government of New Spain in picture 2?

6 Is picture 2 useful as a piece of historical evidence? Give reasons for your answer.

7 You are one of the following:
(a) Cortés
(b) the grandchild of an Eagle Knight
(c) the Viceroy of New Spain.

Design an illustrated page for a book called *The History of New Spain*.

8 What were the advantages and disadvantages of Spanish rule for the Indians?

9 What benefits might the Spanish claim they had brought to Mexico? Do you believe them?

10 Were the Indians better off after the conquest? Explain your answer.

3 The work of the friars in New Spain

Seaport 1558

Seaport is a bustling, busy port on the south coast of England. Seaport ships sail across the channel to Holland and France carrying wool. From Antwerp they bring back hops, sugar, glass, straw hats, prunes, paper, spectacles, combs and expensive cloth.

The discovery of the New World has brought new opportunities to the town. Spices and luxury goods have begun to arrive in large quantities. Seaport captains looking for large profits have started to attack Spanish treasure fleets. Seaport has become rich.

Merchants have built new warehouses near the waterfront to store the goods. More people have moved into the town, hoping to share the new wealth. The town has grown. Houses now sprawl well beyond the old medieval walls.

Lots of small shops have sprung up. They sell imported luxury goods, as well as the goods needed to supply the ships and sailors. On the outskirts of the town, there are several small factories producing iron goods. There is a busy shipyard. There are also many inns.

The Russell family

Mr Russell, a Welsh farmer, died 2 months ago. He left a wife, Ann, a young, intelligent and hardworking woman, and 2 children. Margaret, aged 14, is a strong, clever girl. Her brother Martin is 12. He is strong and cheerful but not very bright. Mr Russell's brother, John, lives in Seaport. He is a printer. Imagine you are one of the children.

2 houses and an inn

and on the other side of the street . . .

a shoemaker's shop

a ropemaker's shop

1 Your mother has decided to move to Seaport. She is clearing up at home, and you have been sent to stay with Uncle John. On your first day at Seaport you go down to the dock to see a ship which has just come in.

Look at the picture on the opposite page. This shows the scene as the ship is being unloaded. Write a letter home to your mother, describing what is going on. Tell her what a busy and exciting place Seaport is.

2 Explain how each of the following could do well living in Seaport:
sailor; merchant; thief; carpenter; blacksmith; beggar; lawyer; priest; tailor; doctor

3 Your mother wants to buy somewhere to live, and also a small business. The best area seems to be Shore Street, near the docks. The picture at the top of this page shows the street. On one side of the street there are 2 houses and an inn for sale. On the other side there are 2 shops for sale.

Number 1 Shore Street (on the left). A large house owned by a lawyer who died of the plague 3 years ago. It has been empty ever since, and will need repairs. It costs £45.

Number 2 Shore Street (in the middle). A much smaller house, but in good condition. It is occupied by an armourer and his family who are moving to London. It costs £50.

Number 3 Shore Street (on the right). An inn, always full of sailors and doing a very good trade. It has several public rooms, a large kitchen and cellars. There are 6 bedrooms. You could use some and rent others to guests. The inn costs £190.

Number 10 Shore Street is a shoemaker's shop. It seems to be doing a good trade. The cobblers say they will stay on and work for the new owner. The shop costs £100 and the stock (leather, tools etc.) costs £40.

Number 12 Shore Street is a ropemaker's shop. It is very busy. Only one of the workers wants to stay on. The others are going on a voyage of exploration. However, there are plenty of workers in the town looking for jobs. The shop costs £120 and the stock (ropes, hemp, tools) costs £35.

After the sale of your father's farm, your mother will have £200 to buy a new home and a business.

Choose the best way for your mother to spend her £200. Write a paragraph explaining to her why that is the best choice.

4 What do you think will be some of the problems of living in Shore Street?

5 Do you think you will be happy in Seaport?

6 Draw a sign to hang outside the new business.

The Queen goes on Tour

The Court

It is August and Queen Elizabeth is on tour. The procession of 400 carts and 2,000 pack-horses travels slowly, covering only 10 miles a day, but it will soon be nearing Seaport. Everywhere she goes there is a public holiday. Huge crowds turn out to cheer her.

She stays in the houses of great nobles. Food for the many courtiers is bought on the journey. They are fed at the Queen's expense. They eat huge quantities of food. At Cowdray Park, near Windsor, 3 oxen and 140 geese were cooked for Sunday breakfast.

The Queen's hosts compete to put on the best entertainment. The picture shows the pageant put on by the Earl of Hertford, when the Queen was staying in his house at Elvetham in Hertfordshire.

The Queen stayed for 3 days. In preparation, 300 workers enlarged the house, put up many new buildings and dug a lake. This was shaped like a half moon. In it were built 3 islands. One was shaped like a ship, one like a fort and one like a snail.

When she arrived, the Queen was greeted by a poet who recited Latin verses. She was led into the house by girls who sang and spread flowers on the path. The following afternoon, she went down to the lake, where she saw a pageant which included characters from Greek legends. Strange sea creatures towed a boat across the lake.

The next day, musicians dressed as country people sang at Elizabeth's window. In the evening, there was a spectacular fireworks display. This was followed by a banquet.

1 What were the advantages of the tour to each of the following?
    the Queen
    the nobles she stayed with
    the ordinary people of England

2 Look at the picture of events at Elvetham and explain what is happening.

Hints for the exercise opposite
What the Queen likes:
cards, chess, dancing, hawking, hunting, music, riding, singing, walking, beautiful clothes, plays, pageants and amusing conversation.

SQUARE DESCRIPTION	POSSIBILITIES	COST
1 Waste ground	Build summer house and new garden. Invite villagers to camp there to greet the Queen. Provide some food.	1 ½
2 Orchard	Demonstration of cider making. Spectacular evening play with fireworks.	½ 1
3 Forest	Stag hunt. Pageant on the theme of the history of England.	½ 1
4 Forest	Chop this down except for some trees which will make the huge pattern 'ER'. Hire musicians, actors and jugglers to perform a play.	 0 1
5 Gardens	Put in fountains for water spectacular. All-night dancing.	1 1
6 House	Build new wing with luxury bedrooms. Redecorate house.	2 1
7 Lake and marsh	Rebuild—create islands and buildings on different themes. Fishing.	2 0
8 Hills	Poets reciting poems in Latin; musicians playing sweet music. The whole court riding round sightseeing and admiring the view.	1 0

You are Lord and Lady Deeshire. Your estate is close to Seaport. The Queen has written to say that she wishes to inspect the fleet at Seaport, and intends to honour you with a visit. You will have to entertain her as well as you can.

What to do

1 Look at the map. It shows your estate.

2 Look at the table. It shows the events you could arrange in each area.

3 You have enough money to feed the household for however long it stays. You must throw a die once to decide how much extra money you have. You can spend all or some of this money enter-taining the Queen. The cost of each item is shown on the table in units.

4 Throw a die to find out how many days the Queen decides to stay.

5 Draw up an illustrated programme to present to the Queen to show what you will do. You must do your best to entertain her even if you are short of money.

6 To help you, read about what the Queen enjoys on the opposite page. You can think up as many extra items as you like as long as they don't cost anything. Remember to allow time for the Queen to eat, sleep and relax.

Justice of the Peace

This picture shows Sir John Petre. He is a Justice of the Peace (J.P.), and a most important person in the county.

As J.P. he has a number of jobs. These are:

1 Controlling and licensing alehouses
2 Maintaining roads and bridges
3 Building jails and poor houses
4 Fixing local wage rates
5 Supervising the whipping of beggars
6 Stopping riots
7 Reporting people who don't go to church.

However, his main task is to judge the cases which appear before him at the *Quarter Sessions*. Really serious cases—murder, manslaughter, rape, forgery, burglary—are sent on to the *Assize Courts* in the county town. There they are heard by a trained judge who travels the country to attend these courts.

Many crimes at this time are punished by death. So at least half of the people condemned to death are tried and sentenced by J.P.s at the *Quarter Sessions*.

You would recognise many of the crimes committed in Elizabethan England. But there were many offences which are no longer crimes. Today, for instance, you would be surprised to be arrested for forgetting to wear a woollen cap on Sunday. In Elizabethan times, if you did this you would be breaking a law passed to help the wool industry. The table below shows some of these Elizabethan crimes, taken from Essex Court records.

Sir John Petre

CRIME	MEANING
Riot	More than 3 people together causing trouble
Disseisin	Unlawful taking of another person's land or property
Barratry	Quarrelling
Rescue	Taking a person or an animal by force
Unlawful games	Playing bowls, backgammon, cards, slide-groat, dice etc. on holy days
Sedition	Encouraging disloyalty to the crown
Inmate	Letting part of your house to someone without a job
Nuisance	Causing floods, bad smells etc. which upset others
Archery	Not practising archery regularly
Trespass	Going into someone else's property without permission
Recusance	Missing church

Document A—1567

Richard Strutt ... keepeth an alehouse against the statute and being forbidden by the justice and constables maintaineth evil rule and receiveth vagabonds, so that there was of late a robbery committed by one that was a vagabond and harboured there in the house of the said Richard Strutt, and also upon St Stephen's day last there was a bloodshed drawn in his house, viz. of one which had a broken head.

Document B—1592

Henry Abbott junior hath drawn blood upon William Clerke and utterly hath maimed and lamed his finger. In the night time he hath in his shirt come out of his house and in the street hath disquieted the watchmen. Being commanded by constables to ward the next day he refused. He hath railed upon divers of his neighbours and them in the most gross terms and speeches greatly abused. Divers and sundry times he hath played at cards, dice, tables and other unlawful games and that very often. He is very much given to contention and moveth great strife and variance between his neighbours and many suits and actions by him have been moved.

Document C—Criminals appearing before the J.P.

1 1582 A man of Great Bursted drove from the pound his own cattle put there because of trespass in the Lord's wood

2 1571 George Jeppes and Thomas Raffe shot with handguns at geese called mallards

3 1588 A common victualler (alehouse keeper) allowed 12 persons to play at cards after midday on a feast day

4 1577 William Gifford for harbouring Francis Gifford a person suspected of having no lands or livelihood

5 1578 Inhabitants of Halstead who threw filth or any strange thing into their gutters

6 1601 James Bardney, pewterer, uttered 3 shillings of mixed metal

7 1576 Mary Cleeve declared the Queen was baseborn and not born to the crown but that another lady was the right inheritor

8 1577 At Brentwood Chapel 30 women pulled Richard Brooke, schoolmaster, out of the chapel and beat him. They resisted arrest holding pitchforks, bills, a piked staff, 2 hot spits, hot water in 2 kettles, 3 bows and 9 arrows, a hatchet, a great hammer and a great sharp stone

9 1585 William Pinder, rector of Stock, a common disturber of the peace and caused discord among his neighbours

10 1594 14 men armed with clubs, swords, armour and guns loaded with powder and shot, broke the doors and windows with axes, and wounded those within and took the house

11 1571 The Vicarage at Great Marplestead raided by 3 males and 6 females who carried away hops

12 1592 15 bargemen from Ware broke the bank of the mill race at Sir Edward Dennye's mill, diverted the stream and beat his servants when they came and ordered the gang to stop

1 Look at Document A.
(a) What job did Richard Strutt do?
(b) What 2 crimes did Strutt commit?
(c) What other crime did this lead to?

2 Look at Document B.
(a) Explain in modern English 6 crimes committed by Henry Abbott.
(b) Which do you think was the most serious crime? Why?

3 Look at Document C.
(a) Complete the table:
(b) Which of the crimes in Document C do you think is the most serious? Why?
(c) If you were J.P. of Seaport which of the criminals listed on Document C would you send to the Assizes?

NO. NAME	CRIME	MODERN EXPLANATION
1 Unknown	Rescue	Stole back his own cattle from the pound
2 George Jeppes Thomas Raffe	Poaching	Shot wild geese

4 Using one or more of these cases as a starting point, write the story of an Elizabethan crime. Draw your own pictures to illustrate it.

5 Why do you think many people carried weapons in the sixteenth century?

Poor People....

The problem of the poor

During Elizabeth's reign there was a great increase in the number of poor people in England because:

1 Bad harvests pushed up the price of food.
2 Monasteries which had given help to the poor had been shut down by King Henry VIII (Elizabeth's father).
3 The rising population meant there were not enough jobs.
4 Prices were rising steadily.
5 Sheep farming had become more popular. This needed fewer workers than ordinary farming, so many farm labourers lost their jobs.

These were the arrangements made for poor people in Seaport.

1 If possible the 'impotent poor' (helpless poor) were looked after in their own homes. They were paid money from the **Parish Poor Rate**. This money was raised by taxes on the people of Seaport. Sick people could be given a licence to become beggars. Children or orphans could be apprenticed to learn a useful trade. There was also an Almshouse in Seaport. Money left in people's wills was used to build this. If poor people could not be looked after at home they could go there.

2 The 'poor by casualty' (accidental poor) were first treated in St Hilda's Hospital. Then they were put into the **Parish Workhouse**. It was stocked with materials like wool, wood and iron. There women spun and men did carpentry. Children were taught useful work and educated.

3 The 'idle poor' were put into the Seaport **Bridewell**. In this 'house of correction' they were forced to work and punished to get rid of their lazy habits.

Many poor people turned to begging to survive. Large bands of beggars, called sturdy beggars, or vagabonds (tramps), wandered round the countryside. They robbed people and often caused fights. Large groups of these desperately poor people could terrorise towns and villages. Several beggars are shown in the pictures opposite.

This is the Poor Law

Part of the Elizabethan Poor Law

'The **impotent poor** [helpless poor] are divided into 3 kinds, that is to say: the fatherless poor man's child; the old, blind and lame; the diseased person by leprosy, dropsy etc.

The **poor by casualty** [accidental poor] are of 3 kinds, that is to say: the wounded soldier; the decayed householder; the greeted with grievous disease.

The **thriftless poor** [idle poor] are 3 kinds in likewise, that is to say: the rioter that consumeth all; the vagabond that will live in no place; the idle person.'

Giving alms

1 Why were the poor considered to be such a nuisance? Why were there more poor people during Elizabeth's reign?

2 What was the difference between the 'deserving poor' and the 'idle poor'?

3 At the top of the opposite page are pictures of beggars. Some use special tricks to get extra sympathy and money. One pretends to be a gentleman down on his luck; one pretends to be mad; one pretends to have dreadful fits. Which is which? Why does one eat soap?

....and Beggars

Beggar lady

Bright Nicholas

Soap eater

Tom O'Bedlam

4 Imagine you are a beggar. Draw a labelled diagram of yourself to show how you could change your appearance to make people feel sorry for you.

5 Sir John Petre is J.P. for Seaport. Like most Elizabethans he believes that the idle poor are poor because they are lazy. They do not deserve help from the parish. Other types of poor people are more deserving.

As J.P., part of his job is to decide who should get help. Today 4 people have applied to him for help from the parish.

Imagine you are Sir John. Your task is to interview the poor people. You must discover what sort of poor people they are—whether they are deserving poor, and what should be done with them. The flow chart will help you.

6 When you have finished your interview, write a detailed account for the court records.
Explain
(a) who the poor people are
(b) why they want help
(c) what you have decided to do, and why.

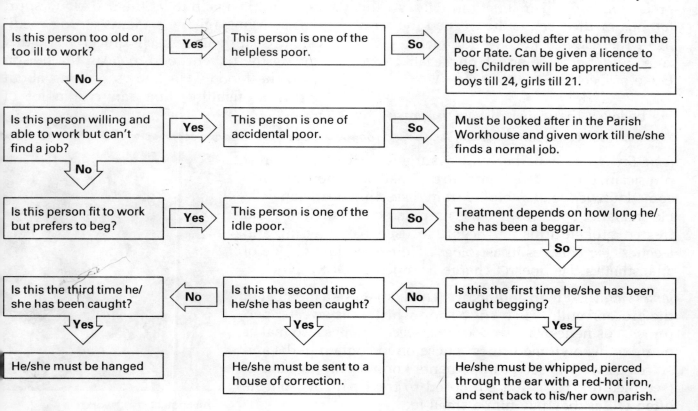

Is this person too old or too ill to work? **Yes →**	This person is one of the helpless poor. **So →**	Must be looked after at home from the Poor Rate. Can be given a licence to beg. Children will be apprenticed—boys till 24, girls till 21.
No ↓		
Is this person willing and able to work but can't find a job? **Yes →**	This person is one of accidental poor. **So →**	Must be looked after in the Parish Workhouse and given work till he/she finds a normal job.
No ↓		
Is this person fit to work but prefers to beg? **Yes →**	This person is one of the idle poor. **So →**	Treatment depends on how long he/she has been a beggar. **So ↓**
Is this the third time he/she has been caught? **← No**	Is this the second time he/she has been caught? **← No**	Is this the first time he/she has been caught begging?
↓ Yes	**↓ Yes**	**↓ Yes**
He/she must be hanged	He/she must be sent to a house of correction.	He/she must be whipped, pierced through the ear with a red-hot iron, and sent back to his/her own parish.

Doctor

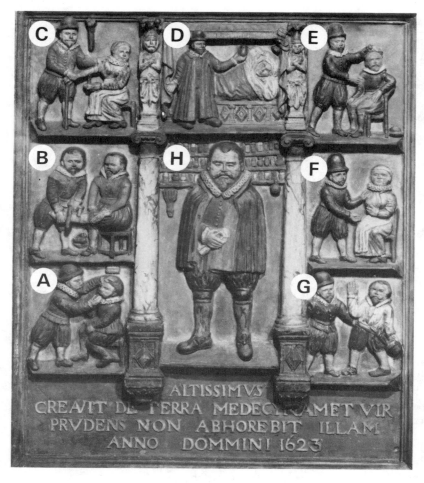

This is actually a signboard dated 1623, but it gives a good idea of the activities of an Elizabethan doctor. The Latin inscription underneath says, 'The highest created medicine from the earth, and a sensible man will not be afraid of it'

Dr Swayne is a **physician** (doctor) with a degree from Padua University in Italy. At this famous medical school he learned the art of medicine. He has a licence to practise medicine, and he is personal physician to the Duke of Deeshire.

He believes that most disease is caused by poison in the blood. His main cures are bleeding (cutting a vein to let the bad blood spurt out); purging (giving patients strong medicine to clear their stomachs quickly); and diet (giving the patient food to clean the poison from the blood). He knows nothing about germs. Consulting him can cost a lot of money.

John Spencer is a barber and a **surgeon**. He is not a real physician, but he has a licence to do small operations. He has some knowledge of anatomy from dissecting dead convicts. He can lance abcesses. He has amputated several limbs and treated broken arms and legs. He used blood-letting and leeches. He believes in astrology. He has no knowledge of anaesthetics. He doesn't charge as much as Dr Swayne.

James Hardwicke is an **apothecary** (chemist). He is a member of the grocers' guild. He owns a shop which sells sweets, perfumes, cosmetics, fancy goods and spices. James also makes many of his own medicines. These often contain herbs and spices as well as secret ingredients known only to himself (see picture). He is not supposed to treat patients, but he often will if they pay him a small fee.

An apothecary at work

Mother Comfort

Mother Comfort is a **wise woman**. She is a well-known character in the town. Mother Comfort has been a midwife. This is one of the most respected and sought-after careers for a woman. She has a licence from the bishop to deliver babies. To get this, she swore an oath not to use any kind of witchcraft or chanting while working.

When delivering babies she always has clean hands and nails. She never wears rings or bracelets, and always puts plenty of butter on her hands.

She also offers advice and help to anyone who asks her. She knows many useful rhymes and sayings which are easy to remember, like these:

'Roots of comfrey beaten out
And spread on thick will ease the gout'
'Cleanliness is next to godliness'

All her medicines are made from herbs like aniseed, mint, lavender, bay, sage, thyme, parsley and liquorice. She grows all these in her garden.

She also has lots of little charms, like dried flowers or rhymes on paper, which are said to help patients. She charges a very small fee or a basket of vegetables.

1 Look at the picture on the opposite page of a doctor at work. Your teacher may help you. Match each of the following activities with the correct letter on the picture: amputates a leg; says goodbye; treats a tumour of the breast; blood-letting; examines urine; extracts a tooth.

What do you think is being shown in the other pictures?

2 Is this doctor licensed as a physician or a surgeon?

3 Why was blood-letting so widely used by doctors? Do you think it was a sensible treatment? Give your reasons.

4 The following people are patients in Seaport. Choose 6 of them, then say which of the 4 medical people above you would advise them to visit, and explain why. Suggest how each might treat the patient.

(a) A pregnant mother aged 18. It is her first baby. She is very nervous.
(b) A soldier with a bullet in his leg.
(c) A rich merchant's wife with a bad headache.
(d) A cook with toothache.
(e) A young man sick with love for a girl.
(f) A man with dandruff and fleas. He is about to get married.
(g) An old lady with arthritis.
(h) A middle-aged man with a huge wart on his nose.
(i) A woman who spits blood and coughs loudly.

Sea Dog

It is 1577. A group of important citizens of Seaport have raised £1,000 from their own wealth and from other people in the town. They want to invest this money in an enterprise which will bring great wealth to them and to the town. Naturally, since Seaport is such an important port, this venture will be connected with the sea.

There are 2 possibilities. At this moment Francis Drake and Walter Raleigh are in Seaport. Both are well-known sea captains, and each has a plan for a venture and is looking for money. The leading citizens will interview them to decide which one will be given the money they have raised.

The leading citizens:

1 Lady Deeshire: owns huge estates near the town. As a loyal English Protestant she wishes to see an end to Spanish power.

2 Sir William Newey: a rich eccentric who is interested in science, particularly astronomy, geography, and the study of animals and plants.

3 Mistress Jennifer Craig: recently widowed, she has taken over her husband's trading business. She owns many warehouses near the waterfront.

4 James Wellbeloved: a Puritan interested in starting a new community away from Catholics.

5 Lady Eleanor Chambers: used to be a lady-in-waiting to the Queen but is out of favour, and suspected of being a Catholic. Wants to help any enterprise which will bring glory to England without harming Spain.

6 Andrew Northedge: a merchant close to ruin. He will invest the last of his money in anything that will restore his fortune.

The interviews

1 The class is divided into several groups of 6 pupils or less.

2 Each pupil takes the role of a leading citizen. You interview, discuss and write reports *as this character*.

3 The whole class interviews each sea captain. Take notes. Anyone can ask questions to find out:
(a) Exactly what each of them is proposing
(b) How each of them is going to spend the money
(c) What chance of success each venture has
(d) What profits and benefits will come to Seaport
(e) How *you* will benefit.

4 In your groups you then discuss who you think should get the money. When you have decided you take a vote (once only).

5 Write a report (in character) describing the venture that got the most votes. Explain why *you* did or did not vote for it. Say what you think Seaport and *you* may gain from this venture.

● Draw a poster to be put up in the town to advertise 'The Seaport Venture'

Francis Drake

You are a well-known sea captain from Seaport. You began your career on a merchant ship. You were such a brilliant captain that you were given the ship by the owner. Since then you have made a good deal of money. You have sunk many Spanish ships and stolen their gold. You have been on a number of voyages to the New World and are a skilled navigator. Your plan is to sail round the world. This means going round the southern tip of South America and crossing the Pacific.

You want to get together a strong expedition to raid the Spanish settlements on the west coast of America, which no English person has seen. You expect to bring back considerable gold through raiding Spanish towns in the New World.

The Queen and her courtiers have already promised you soldiers and several thousand pounds. This will be enough to buy 3 large ships. You need extra money from Seaport to buy and fill a store ship. This will carry food and gunpowder on the journey out and gold on the journey back. You expect to seize at least £500,000 in gold. The Queen will keep half, but Seaport should get £50,000.

You will also find new places and new routes for trade. Ferdinand Magellan sailed round the world 50 years ago, but he was Portuguese. Your expedition will now bring wealth and glory to England.

Walter Raleigh

You are rich and have friends at court. You have fought against Catholics in Holland and Ireland.

You believe that there are great opportunities in North America, which have not yet been explored by the Spanish.

You want to set up a company to start a settlement on the east coast of America. Your colony will be called Virginia. You will ask for people to volunteer to start a new life in a new world. You believe that there is great wealth to be found in North America. This could be the start of an English Empire like New Spain.

It is even possible that the colonists may find a north-west passage round the top of America to Cathay. This would bring great wealth to England. You have read about the voyage of Martin Frobisher last year when he searched for the North-West Passage. He was driven back by ice, but saw people who looked like the inhabitants of Cathay.

You need 2 ships with crews to find a suitable site. You also need to buy equipment and tools for building the settlement.

The Queen is very interested in your plan, and has provided money to equip one of your ships. You will use the money from Seaport to buy this second ship with a crew and all the equipment and tools you need.

Struggle in Europe

This game is about the situation in Europe between 1540 and 1587. You will be working in groups, playing the roles of either England or Spain.

This was a time of great religious rivalry. For centuries the only religion in Europe had been Catholicism. However, in the last 50 years a new religion had developed in Europe, Protestantism.

In some areas of Europe, Catholics and Protestants were fighting. There was a civil war going on in France, for instance. Another religious problem came from the Turks. The Turkish Empire had grown extremely large in the last 50 years. The Turks were not Christians. They were Muslims. They were very warlike and wanted to invade Europe.

Rules

1 You will be divided into groups. Each group will play either England or Spain.

2 Read the information about the world on these pages, and about your country on page 60.

3 The game has 6 rounds. Each round begins with your teacher reading the *world news* for that round. Listen carefully. Take notes.

4 When you have heard the news, each group decides which move it will make in that round. *You can make only one move per round* (*either* an open move *or* a secret move). You must *discuss* this with other members of your group. You will be allowed about 5 minutes. You may talk to other groups at this stage.

5 Each group has one *secret move* per round. Your teacher will tell you what this is. It must be kept secret from your enemies.

6 When all groups have decided which move they will make, they write the number of the round and the letter of the move on a piece of paper, and give it to the teacher. You will then be told your score.

7 Points are awarded for moves which will make your country stronger, or help you gain an advantage over your enemies.

8 The winning group will be the one with the most points at the end of round 6.

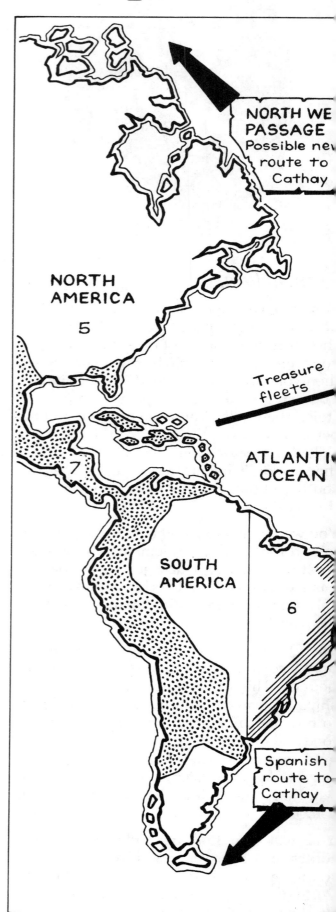

NORTH WE
PASSAGE
Possible new
route to
Cathay

NORTH
AMERICA
5

Treasure
fleets

ATLANTIC
OCEAN

SOUTH
AMERICA
6

Spanish
route to
Cathay

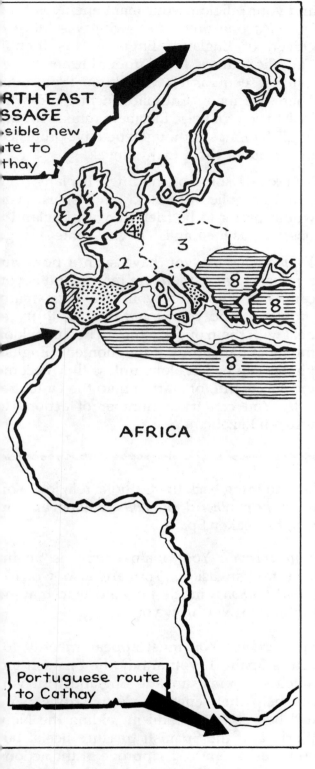

NORTH EAST PASSAGE
possible new route to Cathay

AFRICA

Portuguese route to Cathay

1 **England**
Not very strong at this time. Ruled by Elizabeth I, who is always short of money. The country is steadily becoming Protestant.

2 **France**
Divided and weakened by civil war between the Protestants in the south and the Catholics in the north.

3 **The Holy Roman Empire**
Made up of hundreds of small states. Ruled by the Holy Roman Emperor but very divided. Many Protestant states in the north. Mostly Catholic in the south. Constantly attacked by the Turks.

4 **The Netherlands**
Part of the Spanish Empire. The Dutch in the north are Protestant, and have rebelled against Spanish rule. They are quite rich, but do not have a strong army. They have a good number of ships.

5 **North America**
An unknown land, inhabited by fierce tribes. No Europeans there. It might be an area for settlement.

6 **Portugal**
A Catholic country. Not very big, but Portuguese explorers have opened many profitable new sea routes to the Far East. The Portuguese have settled in Brazil.

7 **Spain**
The most powerful Catholic power in the world. It has a very strong army and navy. It has an Empire in Europe. The Spanish recently conquered the New World. They have looted it and send regular treasure fleets back to Spain.

8 **The Turks**
A powerful Muslim Empire. It has been growing recently and threatens eastern Europe. The Turks are unfriendly, and a threat to trade in the Mediterranean.

1 Look at each of the marked areas on the map and read the information about each one. You may have some questions to ask your teacher.

2 Is any other Catholic country likely to help Spain? Give your reasons.

3 Is any other Protestant country likely to help England? Give your reasons.

4 England has a strong navy. How could this be used best to get money for England?

5 Why might England be interested in exploring the North-West or North-East Passages?

Spain and England

Philip II

You are King of Spain, which is the strongest power in Europe. You have a huge navy, and the largest army in the world.

Your main aims: Your main aim is to defend your huge Empire. You have rich lands in *Italy* which are threatened by the Turks. Their armies are attacking the Holy Roman Empire and their pirate ships are attacking your ships and ports in the Mediterranean.

In the *Spanish Netherlands* Dutch rebels (Protestants) must be stamped out.

Your main concern is with your rich Empire in the *New World*. You want to protect the treasure fleets from attacks by English pirates like Drake.

As a Catholic leader, you also want to spread and defend the *Catholic Religion*. You can use your armies and priests to do this.

Your enemies: Apart from the Dutch rebels and the Turks who threaten your Empire and your religion, your main enemy is England. At one time, your wife was Mary I, Queen of England. England was then a Catholic country. Now, under Elizabeth, her sister, it seems as if it will become Protestant. There are many Catholics in England who look to you for help. Elizabeth refuses to stop English pirates, although you have protested to her about them many times.

You know some of the English plans from your Catholic informers and spies. You would prefer to be friendly with England if possible, as the English navy is quite strong.

Your actions: As you have such a powerful army and navy, there are many actions you can take. However, you also have many problems, and you would be wise to try to deal with them one at a time. The Turks look the most dangerous at the moment. English pirates can be left alone unless they become too successful, or start to help the Dutch rebels. You can try a number of actions to weaken Elizabeth.

Elizabeth

You are Queen of England. At this time England is not a very strong country. There are 2 *main problems*. The first is lack of money. The second is to do with religion. England was a Catholic country under your sister, Mary I. But you are not a Catholic. You want a peaceful Protestant England. England has 2 *big advantages*. The first is that the English navy is strong, and led by brave captains. The second is that you are a very clever queen, deeply loved by your people.

Your main aims: Your first aim is to *get more money*. You are annoyed that Spain and Portugal have divided the world between them. This stops you having an empire of your own. But you have an excellent navy. Your captains are very experienced in raiding and piracy. The Spanish treasure fleets are a tempting target.

Your second aim is to *protect England.* You fear that the Spanish may try to invade England to bring back the Catholic religion. You must *help other Protestants* whenever you can, to weaken Spain.

Your enemies: Your main enemy is Spain. You fear invasion. You are also worried about *Catholics* inside England who may be plotting to overthrow you.

Your actions: You must appear friendly towards Spain. If you annoy the Spanish too much, they may invade England. But you can help their enemies. Your strong navy will be very successful in raiding the New World and the Spanish treasure fleets, but you must seem to disapprove of the actions of the sea dogs. You must try to stay friendly with the Spanish for as long as you can, while working secretly against them. Direct attacks on Spain would be very dangerous, and should only be carried out in emergencies. If a major Spanish attack threatens, you must bring all your ships back to defend England.

Round

	1	2	3	4	5	6
	Send more soldiers to Holland	Attack the Turks	Organise a Crusade against Turks	Attack the Turks	Send more soldiers to Holland	Attack and burn Dutch towns
b	Send Catholic priests to Holland	Build more forts in the New World	Pay money to French Catholics	Make a peace treaty with other Catholic countries	Execute Dutch Protestants in Holland	Build coastal forts to defend Spain
c	Build a fleet to send to the Mediterranean	Send more soldiers to the New World	Withdraw soldiers from Holland	Ask Elizabeth to execute sea dogs	Recall ships from the New World	Prepare a huge fleet to attack England
d	Build a fleet to send to the New World	Send more ships to the New World	Call all ships back to Spain	Send more ships to the New World	Send more ships to the New World	Send more ships to the New World
e	Secret 1	Secret 2	Secret 3	Secret 4	Secret 5	Secret 6

Round

	1	2	3	4	5	6
a	Stop and search ships in the English Channel	Seize Spanish possessions in England	Send money to Spain to show friendship	Ask Spanish ambassador to leave England	Raid the New World	Move whole fleet to Scotland
b	Send whole fleet to search for Eldorado	Send money to the Dutch	Send some ships to help the Dutch	Publicly reward sea dogs	Recall all fighting ships to England	Go on tour of main ports to reward sailors
c	Allow Dutch refugees into England	Draw up plans to build coastal forts	Raid Spanish treasure fleets in New World	Raid Spanish towns in New World	Settle the New World	Recall all fighting ships to England
d	Secret 1	Secret 2	Secret 3	Secret 4	Secret 5	Secret 6

The Armada 1588

The Pope Consulting with his Cardinalls & Contributing a Million of Gold towards the Charge of the Armada —

Don Alphonso Duke of Medina, Cheife Comander of y Spanish Fleete. & John Martin Recalde, a great Seaman.

The Spanish Armada consisting of 130 Shipps whereof 72 were Galleasses and Galeons in wch were 19290 Soulders, 8350 Marriners, 2080 Gally slaves & 2630 great Ordinance. y Navy was 3 whole yeares preparing.

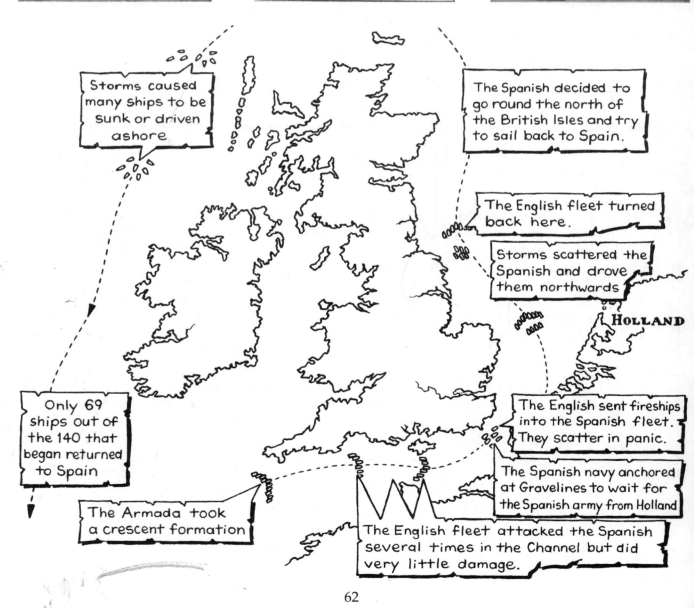

Storms caused many ships to be sunk or driven ashore

The Spanish decided to go round the north of the British Isles and try to sail back to Spain.

The English fleet turned back here.

Storms scattered the Spanish and drove them northwards

HOLLAND

Only 69 ships out of the 140 that began returned to Spain

The Armada took a crescent formation

The English sent fireships into the Spanish fleet. They scatter in panic.

The Spanish navy anchored at Gravelines to wait for the Spanish army from Holland

The English fleet attacked the Spanish several times in the Channel but did very little damage.

King ♥

e Army of 1000 horse, and
2000 Foot, which y͘ Earle of
icester comanded when hee
ched his Tents att Tilbury

VI ♠

More then halfe y͘ Spanish

Fleet Taken and Sunck

III ♠

Queene Eliz: w͘th Nobles and
Gentry and a great number
of people giving God humble
thanks in S͘t Pauls Church.
and having set upp the Ensignes
taken from the Spaniards.

The Spanish plan: In July 1588 the Armada sailed. It contained about 110 fighting ships and about 40 supply ships. It also carried 30,000 soldiers and sailors with much equipment. It was to sail up the English channel to meet a Spanish army of 25,000 from Holland, led by the Duke of Parma. The fleet would then sail up the Thames and capture London. Philip, King of Spain, believed the Catholics in England would rise up and support his invasion.

English defences: The English had about 100 ships led by Lord Howard of Effingham. Thousands of beacons had been built on hill tops, to carry the news of a Spanish fleet inland.

The Channel: As the Armada entered the Channel they took up a crescent formation. The most powerful ships on the outside protected the weaker ships in the centre. The faster English ships chased them. There were 3 main English attacks. Several Spanish ships were captured, but the main Armada remained together.

Fireships: The Armada anchored at Gravelines to wait for a large Spanish army coming from Holland. But this was delayed by Dutch attacks. The English sailed 8 old ships filled with gunpowder and burning wood into the Spanish fleet. The Spanish panicked and cut their anchor ropes. The English attacked again.

Storm: The weather began to turn stormy. The Armada was driven into the North Sea. The English continued to attack until they were forced by the bad weather to return to port. The Armada tried to sail round Scotland to return home. 45 of the ships sank. Only 3,000 sailors survived. The rest drowned or died of thirst.

A fireship

Armada Exercises

A description of English Prepara[tions]

'The greatest and strongest ships of the who[le]
she sent unto Plymouth . . . The number of the
was about an hundred . . . On land likewise th[rough]
out the whole realm, soldiers were muster[ed and]
trained in all places and were committed unto th[e]
resolute and faithful captains . . . There was at
. . . a mighty army encamped and on both side[s of the]
river fortifications were erected. Unto the said
came in proper person the Queen's most loyal
ty. Also there were other such armies levied
land.'

The · Invincible · Armado · in 88.   F·H·

1 What reasons did Philip II have for launching the Armada?

2 Using the information on pages 62–64 to help you, explain what the English defence plan was. Mention Plymouth, Tilbury, beacons, ships, soldiers.

3 Explain why the attack on England failed.

4 Design a medal to celebrate this famous victory. Use one of the following slogans: 'God breathed and they were scattered' or 'The Spanish Fleet – it came and went'.

5 Imagine you are a diver. You have found the wreck of an Armada ship. It is almost whole, and you suspect much of its contents will be well preserved by the mud in which it is buried. Explain what you would hope to find in the wreck, and why these things would be useful to a historian studying the Elizabethan period.